麦格希 中英双语阅读文库

一样的生活，不一样的文化

【美】德雷瑟 (Dresser, N.) ● 主编

宋凯静 ● 译

麦格希中英双语阅读文库编委会 ● 编

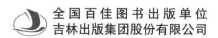

全国百佳图书出版单位
吉林出版集团股份有限公司

图书在版编目（CIP）数据

一样的生活，不一样的文化 / (美) 德雷瑟
(Dresser, N.) 主编; 宋凯静译; 麦格希中英双语阅读文
库编委会编. -- 2版. -- 长春: 吉林出版集团股份有限
公司, 2018.3（2022.1重印）
（麦格希中英双语阅读文库）
ISBN 978-7-5581-4742-5

Ⅰ.①一··· Ⅱ.①德··· ②宋··· ③麦··· Ⅲ.①英语—
汉语—对照读物②文化—概况—美国 Ⅳ.①H319.4：G

中国版本图书馆CIP数据核字(2018)第046064号

一样的生活，不一样的文化

编：麦格希中英双语阅读文库编委会
插　　画：齐　航　李延霞
责任编辑：沈丽娟
封面设计：冯冯翼
开　　本：660mm×960mm　1/16
字　　数：220千字
印　　张：9.75
版　　次：2018年3月第2版
印　　次：2022年1月第2次印刷

出　　版：吉林出版集团股份有限公司
发　　行：吉林出版集团外语教育有限公司
地　　址：长春市福祉大路5788号龙腾国际大厦B座7层
电　　话：总编办：0431-81629929
　　　　　发行部：0431-81629927　0431-81629921(Fax)
印　　刷：北京一鑫印务有限责任公司

ISBN 978-7-5581-4742-5　定价：35.00元

| 前 言 *PREFACE*

英国思想家培根说过：阅读使人深刻。阅读的真正目的是获取信息，开拓视野和陶冶情操。从语言学习的角度来说，学习语言若没有大量阅读就如隔靴搔痒，因为阅读中的语言是最丰富、最灵活、最具表现力、最符合生活情景的，同时读物中的情节、故事引人入胜，进而能充分调动读者的阅读兴趣，培养读者的文学修养，至此，语言的学习水到渠成。

"麦格希中英双语阅读文库"在世界范围内选材，涉及科普、社会文化、文学名著、传奇故事、成长励志等多个系列，充分满足英语学习者课外阅读之所需，在阅读中学习英语、提高能力。

◎难度适中

本套图书充分照顾读者的英语学习阶段和水平，从读者的阅读兴趣出发，以难易适中的英语语言为立足点，选材精心、编排合理。

◎精品荟萃

本套图书注重经典阅读与实用阅读并举。既包含国内外脍炙人口、耳熟能详的美文，又包含科普、人文、故事、励志类等多学科的精彩文章。

◎功能实用

本套图书充分体现了双语阅读的功能和优势，充分考虑到读者课外阅读的方便，超出核心词表的词汇均出现在使其意义明显的语境之中，并标注释义。

鉴于编者水平有限，凡不周之处，谬误之处，皆欢迎批评教正。

我们真心地希望本套图书承载的文化知识和英语阅读的策略对提高读者的英语著作欣赏水平和英语运用能力有所裨益。

丛书编委会

Contents

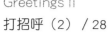

1

Clothing

My name is Linh. I'm an eighteen-year-old girl. My *ethnic background* and native language are Vietnamese. This is a story about what happened to me on my first day of school in America. I was nine years old.

A few weeks before school started, my aunt, my uncle, and some of my dad's friends came to visit us and

服饰

我的名字叫林，今年十八岁，是越南裔移民。下面这个故事讲的是我第一天去美国的学校上学时发生的事，当时我九岁。

在学校开学前几个星期，我的姑姑、叔叔，还有爸爸的朋友来我家做客，他们还带来了很多礼物。我发现其中一个盒子里装的是衣服，让我感

ethnic *adj.* 种族的   background *n.* 背景

they brought a lot of presents. I was surprised when I found clothing in one of the boxes. The clothes were nice but ordinary. They weren't special or *fancy* except for one dress. It was a dress of lace. There was lace surrounding the neck and the *sleeves* and lace on the bottom. I was very happy when I saw this dress.

On the first day of school I wanted to look my best and *impress* the other students. I wanted them to make friends with me, so I put on my fancy dress of lace. But when I got to school, all the students *stared at* me. They were laughing and saying something in English. I didn't know why they were doing this. I thought that maybe they had never seen an Asian girl in a dress before or that they wanted to make friends with me but were embarrassed to come over.

In the classroom an American teacher spoke English to me and

到有些吃惊。那些衣服挺好看，但是很普通，除了其中一件之外都没什么特别之处。那是一件带花边的裙子，领口、袖口还有底边都绣着花边，看到它的时候我开心极了！

　　第一天去上学，我想把自己打扮得最漂亮，给别的同学留下很深的印象，希望他们和我交朋友。于是我便穿上了那件别致的花边裙子。可到了学校以后，发现所有同学都盯着我看，他们都笑出声来，并用英语说些什么。我不明白他们为什么这样做，可能他们从没见过穿裙子的亚洲女孩，或者想和我交朋友，但不好意思过来开口和我说话吧。

　　在课堂上，一位美国老师指着我的衣服，用英语对我说话，我听不懂

---

fancy *adj.* 精美的；花哨的
impress *v.* 给……留下印象

sleeve *n.* 袖子
stare at 凝视；盯住

pointed at my dress, but I didn't know what she was saying so I just smiled. The whole morning she didn't let me walk around or stand up. I had to sit all the way in the last row in the back of the room. During lunch, when all the other students had gone, an Asian teacher came into the room. The minute she saw me she spoke to me in Vietnamese. She told me that I shouldn't wear a *nightgown* to school, that in America people only wear nightgowns to sleep! I was so embarrassed that I almost burst into tears. That morning when I left home, I thought I looked good, but I didn't. Instead, I embarrassed myself on my first day of school. I felt like not going to school anymore.

This *embarrassment* taught me not to try to impress others or I might end up making a fool out of myself. I also learned the difference between a fancy dress and a nightgown!

她的话，所以只是一个劲儿地微笑。整个上午她都没让我走动或站起来，我只好一直坐在教室最后一排。吃午饭的时候，所有同学都走了。一位亚洲老师走进来。一看见我，她便用越南话对我说，我不该穿一件睡袍来上学，那是美国人睡觉时才穿的东西！我当时太难为情了，差点儿哭了出来。早上从家走的时候我以为自己看上去很漂亮，可根本不是那么回事。正相反，第一天去学校就把自己搞得很难堪，真想再也不来上学了。

这件尴尬的事教会了我一个道理，不要总想着给别人留下深刻的印象，因为结果有可能是自己出丑。另外还了解了漂亮衣服和睡袍之间的区别！

nightgown n. 睡衣

embarrassment n. 窘迫；难堪

Clothing Customs

I am a science *professor*. I teach at a university in the United States. Students call me Professor Singh. One day, my wife and I wanted to go out for dinner. We wanted to try a new restaurant.

When we got to the restaurant, the manager asked me to *take off* my hat. I

衣着习俗

我是一位在美国大学任教的自然科学教授，学生们称呼我为"辛格教授"。有一天，我和妻子去外面吃饭，我们想尝试一家新餐厅。

我们到了餐厅，结果那里的经理让我把帽子摘下来。我当时很生气，

---

professor *n.* 教授   take off 脱下；拿掉

was angry. I told him it was not a hat and I could not remove it. The manager would not listen. He said that I had to remove my hat or he would not serve us food. My wife and I left the restaurant.

In the United States, men take off their hats. This shows good manners. It is a sign of respect. The manager wanted his customers to use good manners in his restaurant. He felt that Professor Singh did not show him respect.

Professor Singh is a *Sikh* from India. Sikh men must wear a *turban* at all times. Their turbans are symbols of pride. For a Sikh, removing his turban is *disgraceful*. Professor Singh wore his turban because of his *religion*. He would not take off his turban to eat in the restaurant.

告诉他那不是帽子，我也不能把它摘掉。可他不听，说如果我不摘帽子的话就不为我们提供食物。于是我们就离开了那家餐厅。

在美国，男人摘帽是为了表示礼貌，也是一种尊敬别人的标志。经理希望客人在进入餐厅时能表现得彬彬有礼，而他觉得辛格教授对他不尊重。

辛格教授是来自印度的锡克教教徒，信仰该教的男子必须时刻佩戴头巾，这种头巾是尊严的象征，对他们来说，摘下头巾意味着耻辱。辛格教授戴头巾是出于宗教原因，他不会因为进餐厅吃饭而摘下头巾的。

Sikh *n.* 锡克教教徒   turban *n.* 锡克教教徒或穆斯林的头巾
disgraceful *adj.* 丢脸的   religion *n.* 宗教

3

Table Manners

My name is Eskinder. I was born in *Ethiopia*, but now I live in the United States. My wife is American. Her name is Lucy. My best friend is Isaac. He recently moved here from Ethiopia. One day, he invited us to eat Ethiopian food in his home.

餐桌礼仪

我的名字叫埃斯金德，出生于埃塞俄比亚，但现在生活在美国。我的妻子是个美国人，名字叫露西。我最好的朋友伊萨克，最近刚刚从埃塞俄比亚来美国。有一天他邀请我们去他家品尝埃塞俄比亚菜。

Ethiopia *n.* 埃塞俄比亚

Lucy wasn't worried. She knew many Ethiopian eating customs. She knew how to eat with her fingers. She knew how to use our bread. We call it injera. We use it like a spoon to scoop up food.

That night Isaac made Ethiopian *stew*. At the table, Isaac took a piece of injera. He scooped up some stew with the injera. Then Isaac *held out* the food and put it into Lucy's mouth. Lucy was surprised. She didn't know what to do.

In Ethiopia, to start a meal, the host takes some food and holds the food up to the guest's mouth. The guest eats this food from the host's hand. Lucy did not know this Ethiopian eating custom. Isaac was making Lucy an honored guest, but she did not understand.

Americans do not eat food from someone else's hand. Isaac did not know this. He did not know that Lucy would be surprised.

露西对此并不担心，她了解很多埃塞俄比亚的饮食习俗，知道如何用手来吃饭，也知道怎么来用我们的面包，我们叫作"injera"，是像勺子一样用来舀食物的。

那天晚上伊萨克做了埃塞俄比亚的浓汤。吃饭时他拿起一片"injera"，用它舀起一些汤，然后递过来，放进了露西的嘴里。露西当时吃了一惊，不知如何是好。

在埃塞俄比亚，正式开始吃饭时，要由主人拿起一些食物，伸到客人面前，客人要从主人的手里接过食物并吃下去。露西不知道这条埃塞俄比亚的饮食习俗。伊萨克是把她当作尊贵的客人，但她却并不明白。

美国人是不会从别人手里接东西吃的。伊萨克也不知道这一点，没想到露西会大吃一惊。

---

stew *n.* 炖煮的菜肴   hold out 伸出

Food Taboos

I am Rafael, a *second-generation* American of *Hispanic* descent. I was born in Los Angeles and have lived there for eighteen years. My neighborhood is largely Hispanic. Being raised in a community that has one main ethnic group is both good and bad. It is good because I *appreciate* my culture. It is bad because I am *ignorant* of other

食物禁忌

我叫拉菲尔，是生活在美国的西班牙裔第二代移民。我出生在洛杉矶，在那里已经生活了十八年。我的邻居大部分都是西班牙移民。在单一种族环境中长大可以说有利也有弊，利在于我可以了解自己的文化，而弊端在于让我无法体会到这个世界上还有别的文化存在。所以

---

second-generation *n.* 第二代　　　　　Hispanic *adj.* 西班牙的
appreciate *v.* 了解；认识　　　　　　ignorant *adj.* 无知的

cultures that inhabit the earth. So, not surprisingly, there was an incident when I experienced culture shock. It happened just recently in the home of Gopal, a friend from India.

One rainy day Gopal, who I have known for five months, *invited* me to his home. On my way there I stopped and bought hamburgers for him and me. However, I did not tell him about the hamburgers.

Gopal's family was eating in the *dining room*. Gopal and I were in the *living room*. I asked him, "Do you mind if I eat some food I bought for us?"

"Go right ahead," he answered. "Here, let's go into the dining room. I'll set a place for you at the table."

不久前我经历了一次文化冲击，也就不足为奇了。这件事发生在我一位来自印度的朋友，古帕尔的家里。

那天下着雨，古帕尔邀请我去他家做客，当时我们认识五个月了。在去他家的路上我给他和自己买了汉堡包，但没有告诉他。

古帕尔的家人正在餐厅吃饭。我们俩待在客厅里，我问他："我买了些东西，咱们一起吃，你看怎么样？"

"好啊，"他说，"走，咱们去餐厅，你坐在那里吃。"

---

invite *v.* 邀请   dining room 餐厅
living room 客厅；起居室

I seated myself at the table. Slowly I placed the bag on the table and *extracted* one hamburger for myself and handed the other one to Gopal. As I sank my teeth into the hamburger, his family abruptly stopped eating their meal and began to stare at me. I asked, "Enjoying your meal?"

Not one person answered me. Their stares and the silence that accompanied the stares sent *chills* through my body. I was *confused*.

Finally, after about two minutes, Gopal's mother spoke. She said, "You do not know very much about India and our culture. Did you know that in India the cow is considered *sacred*? It is sacred because the Hindu religion made it holy. We don't and can't eat beef."

我在餐桌旁坐下，慢慢地把包放在桌子上，从里面取出一个汉堡包给自己，然后又递给古帕尔一个。我刚咬了一口，他的家人都停了下来，开始盯着我看。我问道："你们吃得怎么样？"

没人回应我。他们就那么静悄悄地盯着我，弄得我心里有些发毛，很是糊涂。

最后过了大约两分钟，古帕尔的妈妈开口了，她说："你对印度和我们的文化不太了解。你知道吗，在印度牛是非常神圣的东西，因为印度教把牛奉为神灵，我们不吃，也不能吃牛肉。"

---

extract *v.* 取出

confused *adj.* 困惑的；糊涂的

chill *n.* 害怕；担心

sacred *adj.* 神圣的

She and the family understood that I did not know about *Hinduism*. I listened and learned more about India. My interest was undivided and her information was *rewarding*. As a result of this incident I now think before buying beef products. I keep in mind that other cultures have beliefs that we don't have. I do not think the family, especially Gopal, was affected by the incident. No one *was angry at* me. It is *ironic* that Gopal is presently working at Tommy's Burgers.

她和全家人都理解我对印度教教义的无知。我听了她的话，对印度有了更多的了解。我对此很感兴趣，而她的话也非常有用。经历这件事之后，现在我再买牛肉制品的时候都会先想一想，我会记得世界上还有不同于我们的文化存在。我不觉得他们一家，尤其是古帕尔会受什么影响，没有人对我生气。很有趣的是，古帕尔现在就在汤米汉堡店上班。

Hinduism *n.* 印度教
be angry at 对……发怒

rewarding *adj.* 有益的
ironic *adj.* 令人啼笑皆非的；讽刺的

5

Foodways

My name is Arpi. My family is Armenian, but I grew up in Iran. Now I live in the United States. I am a college student here.

One day, I met some other girls in one of my classes. They were two sisters from *Kuwait*. Their family was also Armenian. I was happy to meet other Armenians. I wanted to be their friend. I invited them to my home the next day.

用餐之道

我叫阿尔佩，是亚美尼亚人，但我在伊朗长大。现在生活在美国，在这里读大学。

有一天，我在一个班上认识了两个女孩，她们是来自科威特的一对姐妹，她们一家也是亚美尼亚人。我很高兴能认识别的亚美尼亚人，想和她们交朋友，于是第二天我便请她们来我家做客。

Kuwait *n.* 科威特

When the girls arrived, we began to talk in a very friendly way. They sat down and I immediately brought them cookies and fruit. Then I served them coffee. They looked confused, but I didn't pay much attention. Suddenly, about twenty minutes after they arrived, they stood up. They said goodbye, and they left!

The sisters and Arpi were all Armenian, but they had some different customs. Arpi grew up in Iran. In Iran, people serve coffee to their guests at the beginning of a visit. The sisters grew up in Kuwait. In Kuwait, people serve coffee at the end of a visit. Arpi served coffee and the sisters thought Arpi wanted them to leave. It was very early in the visit, so they felt *insulted*.

The next day, Arpi spoke to the sisters after class. At first, they didn't want to speak to her. But finally, they explained their custom and Arpi explained hers. Arpi was sorry that her guests felt insulted. She *apologized*. After this, the three girls became good friends.

这两个女孩来了之后，我们开始了友好的交谈。她们刚坐下，我就立刻端上了点心和水果。接着我又给她们倒上咖啡。她们却一脸疑惑的样子，但我没有在意。她们坐了二十分钟左右，就起身告别离开！

这对姐妹和阿尔佩都是亚美尼亚人，但她们却有一些不同的习俗。阿尔佩在伊朗长大，在那里，人们在客人造访之初便为他们倒上咖啡。而那对姐妹则在科威特长大，那儿的人是在来访的最后才喝咖啡。阿尔佩倒咖啡的举动让姐妹俩误以为是想要她们离开。而这时她们才刚来不久，因此觉得受到了侮辱。

第二天下课后，阿尔佩询问姐妹二人是怎么回事，开始的时候她们不想说。但后来还是向她解释了她们的习俗，而阿尔佩也解释了她自己的习俗。阿尔佩因为让客人觉得受到侮辱而十分过意不去，于是向她们道歉。事情过去之后，三个女孩成了非常要好的朋友。

---

insult *v.* 侮辱　　　　　　　　　　apologize *v.* 道歉

Eating Out

I was born in Vietnam and since both of my parents are Chinese, most of the things I do *are based on* Chinese customs. However, I have lived in the United States for a long time so I have also *picked up* many American ways, but I still use my Chinese name, Yen.

The one thing I find very difficult to get used

用餐

我出生在越南，父母都是中国人，所以很多行为处事的方法都是以中国式的习惯为基础的。但是，我在美国已经生活了很久，因此也学会了不少美国的方式，但还是用自己的中国名字，燕。

有一件事我很难适应，就是吃饭时用的餐具。在许多美国的餐馆里

be based on 以……基础；基于   pick up 无意地学会（技术、语言、游戏等）

to is the eating *utensils*. In many American restaurants there are two forks, two spoons, and two knives. I get really confused trying to find out which utensil I should use for which kind of food. And not long ago, I didn't know how to use a knife and fork at all.

In my culture the two items we use for eating are a pair of *chopsticks* and a soup spoon. Chopsticks are long skinny sticks made out of wood called bamboo. We use them to pick up our food. The soup spoon is oval in shape and *is* usually *made out of porcelain*. We use it to sip our soup or to scoop our food.

Two years ago, my boyfriend invited me to the Christmas party given by his company. He told me that it was going to be a dinner

通常都有两副刀叉和两把汤勺。我实在分不清哪种食物该用哪个。不久之前，我连一副刀叉还用不好呢。

在中国的文化里，人们用来进餐的用具有两样，一双筷子和一把汤勺。筷子是用竹子做成的两根细长的小棍，用它们来夹取食物。汤勺呈椭圆形，通常用陶瓷做成，用它来喝汤或舀食物。

两年前，我的男朋友邀请我去参加他们公司举办的圣诞晚会。他告诉我那是在喜来登酒店举行的晚餐会，所以要穿得正式一些。之前一星期，

utensil *n.* 用具；器皿
be made out of 由······制作

chopstick *n.* 筷子
porcelain *n.* 瓷；瓷器

party at the Sheraton Hotel and that I should dress *formally*. The week before the party, I went shopping for a pretty dress to wear. I had a hard time because I didn't really know how Americans would dress for this *occasion*. Well, luckily for me, a salesgirl gave me her opinion and I found just the right dress. Then came the day of the party. Knowing I was properly dressed, I felt very comfortable. My boyfriend introduced me to his *coworkers*, and we were seated at a table with four other American couples. Then I looked down at my knife and fork, and my heart sank. I had wanted to ask my boyfriend how to use the utensils for what I called "Eating the Western Way". But I had been so worried about what to wear that I had forgotten. Now, seated at the table with the other couples, I would have to figure out the utensils for myself. Everything went fine until the lady who was sitting next to me noticed that I kept watching what

---

我去买了一件漂亮的衣服准备晚会时穿。这可把我难坏了，因为不知道美国人在这种场合会穿什么样的衣服。幸运的是，一位售货员小姐给了我一些建议，帮我找到了合适的服装。晚会那一天终于到了，因为知道自己的穿着很合体，所以我感觉很轻松。男友把我介绍给他的同事，然后我们和其他四对美国夫妇在一张餐桌旁就座。我低头看了一眼刀叉，心一下子沉了下去！我本来打算来之前请教男朋友我所谓的如何使用西餐中的餐具，但一直忙于考虑穿什么衣服，就把这件事忘了。现在可好，和别人坐在一起，我得自己弄明白这些东西怎么用。一切还算顺利，直到旁边的女士发

---

formally *adv.* 正式地　　　　　　　　　occasion *n.* 场合
coworker *n.* 同事

everyone was doing and switching my fork and knife from one hand to another. She started to laugh and said, "Oh dear, don't be so *nervous*. Let me show you how to use your knife."

At this point my face was red and I didn't know what to say. Usually Chinese people aren't allowed to have a knife on the table. I was still a little scared to hold the knife and now I was also nervous and embarrassed about the whole situation. I *ended up* letting my boyfriend cut the steak for me. As for the lady who was sitting next to me, I was too embarrassed to look at her or thank her for offering to help.

Since then, my boyfriend has taken me to many American restaurants. Not only have I gotten used to eating the food, but he has taught me how to eat the Western way. Now I have no problem handling my knife and fork, but it makes me smile sometimes when I think of how embarrassing it once was.

现我一直在看别人是怎么做的，并把刀叉在手里摆弄来摆弄去。她笑了，对我说："哦，亲爱的，别紧张，我来教你怎么用刀。"

就在那一瞬间，我的脸唰的一下红了，不知该说什么好。通常来说，中国人在餐桌上是不能用刀的，我当时手里拿着刀，心里还是有些害怕。直到今天一想起那天的情形还会感觉有些紧张和尴尬。后来还是让男友帮我切的牛排。至于身旁那位女士，我太难为情了，没敢看她，也忘了表示感谢。

从那以后，男朋友带我去了很多美国餐厅。使我不仅适应了所吃的食物，还教我怎样吃西餐。现在我用起刀叉来已经没有问题了，但有时回想起当初曾经那样的尴尬，还是会令我不禁微微一笑。

---

nervous *adj.* 紧张不安的　　　　　　end up 结束

CULTURE JOURNEYS

7

Guests and Hosts

My name is Tai and I was born in the southern part of China. After receiving a B.A. *degree*, I taught English in Beijing and later became an *interpreter*. Now I am in the United States to get a degree in marketing.

宾与主

我的名字叫泰，出生在中国南方。获得文学学士学位之后，我开始在北京教英语，后来又做了口译。现在在美国进修市场营销学。

---

degree *n.* 学位   interpreter *n.* 口译者

18

MCGRAW-HILL

When I first came to this country, everything seemed strange and different. For example, people often said hello to each other even if they were strangers. In China, only friends say hello when they meet. But of all the cultural differences, one in particular came as a surprise to me. An American friend invited me to a dinner party at her home. A day before the party, I happened to talk to a Chinese friend. He asked me what food I was bringing to the party. I had no idea what he was talking about. In China, the *hosts* prepare all the food and drinks—the only thing that the guests bring is their mouths to eat with. My friend explained to me that the dinner party was a *potluck*. He said that at a potluck dinner party each guest brings food and everybody *shares* the food. It was lucky that I talked to this friend

---

　　刚来到这里时，一切对我来说都是那么新奇而又不同。比方说，即便是陌生人之间也会互相打招呼，而在中国只有朋友见面才会这样。在所有文化差异中，有一件事让我感到特别惊讶。一次一个美国朋友邀请我去她家参加一个晚餐聚会。在那前一天我碰巧和一个中国朋友聊天，他问我准备带什么食物去，我当时不知道他说的是什么意思。在中国，是由主人来负责准备所有的食物和饮品——客人只要带一张嘴去就可以了。朋友跟我解释说，这次晚餐会是一个Potluck，意思是人人都带食物去，大家一起分享。幸亏去之前我和这位朋友聊过，要不然我本来打算带一瓶酒去，那样

---

host *n.* 主人；东道主
share *v.* 分享

potluck *n.* 百味餐

before the dinner. I had just planned to bring a bottle of liquor, and I would have felt embarrassed. Instead, I made some *typical* Chinese food for the potluck, and everyone there really liked it.

As I've learned, many dinners in the United States aren't potlucks. They are more like our Chinese dinners. Guests may bring a bottle of wine or a small gift, but the hosts *provide* the meal. However, I've also come to like the custom of potlucks. Since everyone helps out, potlucks make it easy to have dinner with friends *more often*. This is especially useful since so many women today work and have less time to cook large meals. By now I've explained this custom to many Chinese friends here. And when I'm invited to a potluck, I always do my best to bring some typical Chinese food.

的话就太不好意思了。于是我做了些中国的特色菜带到晚餐会上，所有人都非常喜欢。

后来我逐渐了解到，在美国很多晚餐也不全是这种形式，也和我们中国的差不多。客人通常带一瓶酒或是些小礼物，而由主人来准备膳食。但我还是喜欢上了Potluck 这种习俗。由于人人都动手出力，所以很容易让朋友多在一起聚会。尤其现在有很多妇女都外出工作，没有那么多时间来做大餐。我也给别的中国朋友解释过这件事。再被邀请去参加Potluck时，我都会尽力做些中国特色菜带去。

---

typical *adj.* 特有的；有特色的；典型的   provide *v.* 准备
more often 经常

8

Confusing Phrases

My name is Lorenzo and I was born in *Mexico* City, but I've been living here in the United States for five years. While in the tenth grade I had an incident with my ESL teacher, Mrs. Del Signore.

It all began one night when I

令人困惑的习语

我的名字叫洛伦佐，出生于墨西哥城，在美国已经生活了五年。上十年级的时候，我和英语老师德尔·西格诺雷夫人之间发生了一件事。

有天晚上我做作业一直做到半夜，做完之后把作业本放在餐桌上就去

Mexico *n.* 墨西哥

stayed up until midnight doing homework for the next day. When I finished, I put the homework paper on the dinner table and went to sleep. The next morning I woke up late and was in such a hurry to get to school on time that I forgot to take my homework.

In my ESL class, Mrs. Del Signore said, "Pass your homework to the front of your row." Today, like every day, she used the homework to take *attendance*. So, after a few minutes, she asked, "Lorenzo Gonzales is not here?" I answered, "I'm here."

She turned and looked at me and called me to her desk to ask me about the homework. When I explained what had happened, she answered, "Quit pulling my leg. I want the truth."

I felt my face turning red. What she said didn't make any sense. I wasn't close enough to pull her leg. Besides, she was sitting at her desk, and it would have been *practically* impossible to pull her leg

---

睡觉了。第二天早上起来晚了，急急忙忙跑去上学，忘了带作业本。

英语课上，西格诺雷夫人说："把你们的作业本传到第一排来。"和每天一样，她用作业本来统计出勤情况。过了几分钟，她问道："洛伦佐·冈萨雷斯没来吗？"我回答说："来了。"

她转过身来看着我，叫我到讲台前问话。我把事情解释了一遍，她说：""别拽我的腿'（Quit pulling my leg），我想听真话。"

我的脸一下子红了。她说的话没有什么意义啊！我离她很远，够不到她的腿。再者说，她坐在讲台后面，即使想去拽，也不可能碰到。全班同

---

attendance *n.* 出勤   practically *adv..* 几乎；简直

from under the desk. The whole class looked at her because they did not understand her either. I'm sure I had a *perplexed* look on my face. When Mrs. Del Signore noticed it, she immediately realized the reason and apologized to me and the rest of the class. She explained what she meant by "pulling my leg". She had thought I was kidding her about the homework, that I was just making up a story.

The next day she discussed *idioms*. We were *eager* to learn them, since we could clearly see they would come in handy sooner or later. *As a result* of this experience, to this day whenever I hear an idiom I do not understand, I simply go to my old high school and ask my friend Mrs. Del Signore.

学都看着她，因为他们也不理解。我敢肯定自己当时的表情充满了疑惑。德尔·西格诺雷夫人注意到了，立刻明白是怎么回事，就向我和同学们道歉。她解释了"pulling my leg"的意思，她以为我是在骗她，是我自己编造的理由。

　　第二天她给我们讲解了成语俗语。我们都很愿意学，因为心里清楚早晚这些一定能派上用场。直到今天，每当听到一个不理解的成语时，很简单，我就回母校去问我的朋友，德尔· 西格诺雷夫人。

---

perplexed *adj.* 困惑的；迷惑不解的
eager *adj.* 渴望的

idiom *n.* 成语
as a result 结果

Greetings I

My name is Cristina. I was born in Mexico and came to the United States when I was three months old. Even though we lived in the United States, my parents *raised* my brother, my sisters, and me just as they had been

打招呼（1）

我叫克里斯蒂娜，出生于墨西哥城，三个月大的时候来到了美国。尽管我们在这里生活，但父母教育我们兄弟姐妹的方法还是传统的墨西哥式——即非常严格的纪律。父母告诉我们要特别尊重祖父

---

raise *v.* 抚养；养育

raised in Mexico—with very strict rules. My parents taught us we should *respect* grandparents more than anyone in the world because grandparents had lived the longest. They had more knowledge about life, and no matter what they said, even if it didn't make sense, they were right. We were taught that to *hug* or kiss grandparents was *disrespectful* and that we should greet them by kissing their hands. When you are young, you think that everyone lives and thinks just like you do. Well, I soon found out this isn't true.

My best friend in third grade was the first close friend I had who was raised in the American way. This friend invited me to her birthday party. I was very excited because I had never been invited to a friend's birthday party before.

The day of the party came, and I was happy but at the same

祖母，因为他们年龄最大，人生的阅历最丰富。无论他们说什么，即便没什么意义，也是正确的。问候祖父母的时候不能拥抱或亲吻，那样是不尊重的，应该吻他们的手。要知道，人小的时候总是以为别人的生活方式和想法都和自己的一样。很快我就发现不是那么回事了。

三年级的时候我有一个很要好的朋友，她是我认识的第一个以美国方式长大的朋友。她邀请我去参加她的生日晚会。我很兴奋，因为从来没有被邀请过去这样的场合。

晚会这天到了，我既开心又很紧张，心里盘算着会有什么样的人去参

---

respect *v.* 尊敬
disrespectful *adj.* 无礼的

hug *v.* 拥抱

time very nervous. I thought of all the people who would be there. I wanted her family to like me. Slowly, I walked up to the house. Finally, I got to the door and rang the bell. My friend came running out with a big smile, telling me she was happy that I came. She let me in and *introduced* me to her parents. They smiled and said hello. Then she said, "Come here. I want you to meet my grandpa."

I followed her into the living room where her grandfather was sitting. She introduced us and he *reached out* his hand. He was going to *shake hands*, but I thought he was expecting me to kiss his hand, so I did.

I *noticed* that he looked at me in a strange way, as if he didn't like what I had done. Everyone else in the room looked at me, and my friend started laughing. I was very confused. I didn't know what I

加，并希望她家人会喜欢我。我慢慢地走到她家，最后来到门口，按下门铃。我的朋友面带笑容地跑出来，说我能来她很开心。她迎我进门，然后把我介绍给她父母。他们微笑着和我打招呼。她又说："来吧！我领你去见我爷爷！"

我跟她来到客厅，她爷爷正坐在那里。她做了介绍，然后老人伸出手来。他当时是想和我握手，而我却以为他想让我吻他的手，于是我就那样做了。

我注意到他看我的眼神有些奇怪，似乎不太喜欢我吻他的手。屋子里其他人也都盯着我看。朋友笑了，我心里疑惑不解，不知道自己做错了什

---

introduce *v.* 介绍　　　　　　　　　　　　reach out 伸出
shake hands 握手　　　　　　　　　　　　notice *v.* 注意；觉察

had done wrong. I sat down and tried to figure out what happened. Just then, a little boy ran to my friend's grandfather and *jumped* on his lap. The little boy started to hug and kiss the grandfather. When I saw this, I got up and took the little boy by the hand and said, "No." I guess I said it pretty loudly because the room became very *silent* and all eyes were on me.

The next day at school my friend asked me why I acted so *strangely* at her party. She asked me why I kissed her grandfather's hand and why I told the little boy to get away from his grandfather. I explained my customs to her and she explained hers to me. Fortunately, we stayed very good friends.

么。我坐下来试着想清楚。就在这时，一个小男孩儿跑到老人身边，跳到他腿上，抱住他亲了一下。看到这样的情形，我急忙站起来，抓住那男孩儿的手，说："不！"我想自己当时的声音一定很大，因为屋子里顿时静了下来，所有的眼睛都看着我。

第二天上学时我的朋友问我为什么在她的晚会上表现得如此奇怪，并问我为什么吻她爷爷的手并让小男孩儿离开他的爷爷。我把我们的风俗习惯解释给她听，她也向我解释了她们的风俗。幸运的是，我们仍是好朋友。

---

jump v. 跳
strangely adv. 奇怪地

silent adj. 安静的；沉默的

10

Greetings II

Let me introduce myself. My name is Ben. I was on a business trip in New Zealand. At the airport, I watched families greet each other. Some shook hands. Some hugged and kissed. Some were *serious*. Some were happy. Some were *serious*.

One man arrived from a trip.

打招呼（2）

让我来自我介绍一下，我的名字叫本。一次我去新西兰出差，在机场看到许多家庭在迎接自己的亲人，有的握手，有的拥抱，还有的互相亲吻。有人看上去十分开心，也有的人很严肃。

有一个男人刚下飞机。他看起来像是个商人，穿着深色的西装，拎着

---

serious adj. 严肃的

He looked like a *businessman*. He wore a dark suit and he carried a leather *briefcase*. Another man was there to greet him. They did not shake hands or hug. They pressed their noses together. I was surprised, but this greeting looked very natural for the two men.

The traveler and his friend were *Maori*. When two Maori people greet each other, they press one nose against the other nose. They call this gesture a *hongi*. When two people press noses they share the same breath. This unites them. The hongi means friendship and respect. Some people of Alaska and Canada also press their noses together to greet each other.

一个皮革公文包。另一个男人来接他。他们没有握手也没有拥抱，而是把鼻子碰到了一起。我吃了一惊，可这种打招呼的方式对这两个人来说似乎很正常。

这位旅行者和他的朋友是毛利人。当两个毛利人之间互相打招呼时，他们把鼻子紧贴在一起。他们把这个姿势叫作"hongi"。碰鼻子使得两个人的呼吸到了一处，将他们联系在一起。"hongi"意味着友谊和尊重。在阿拉斯加和加拿大，也有一些人在互致问候时碰鼻子。

---

businessman *n.* 商人
Maori *n.* 毛利人

briefcase *n.* 公文包
hongi *n.* 鼻触礼

Forms of Address

My name is Yuan. As a student in Taiwan for the first ten years of my school life, I learned to *respect* teachers. I was taught that it is not respectful to call teachers by their name, that they should always be addressed by the title "Teacher".

Seven years ago, when I moved to the United States, I entered an ESL class in

---

称呼的方式

我的名字叫园。因为在中国台湾读了十年书，所以学会了尊敬师长。我知道称呼老师的名字是不礼貌的，应该称他们为"老师"。

七年前，我来到美国，在当地一间中学上英语课。同学们都称我们的

---

respect *v.* 尊敬；敬重

a local high school. The students kept calling the teacher "Miss White". I felt that they were being *disrespectful*, but because of my problems with English, I couldn't ask them about it.

Time passed. I found that often when I asked questions, Miss White seemed annoyed and said something, but I was not able to understand what she said. I wondered if I had done something that was not respectful or if somehow I hadn't been a good student. Finally, one day when I raised my hand and said, "Excuse me, Teacher...," Miss White *interrupted* me before I could finish my question. With a not-so-happy face, she said, "Teacher is my title at work. Teacher is not my name. My name is Miss White."

Now I was completely confused. Why would she want me to call her by her name? Why would she get so upset when I was trying to

---

老师为"怀特小姐"。我觉得他们对老师太不尊重了。但因为自己的英文不好，所以没办法问他们。

时间一天天过去了。我发现每当自己问问题的时候，怀特小姐看上去都不太高兴的样子，还说了些什么，但我听不懂。我就想是不是自己做了什么不够尊重她的事，或者自己学习不够努力。最后，有一天我举手说："对不起，老师……"还没有等我说完，怀特小姐就打断了我的话，她的脸色有些难看，说："老师是我工作的头衔，老师不是我的名字，我的名字是怀特小姐！"

这下子我彻底糊涂了。为什么她要我称呼她的名字呢？我在对她表示尊重，可她为什么不高兴呢？我想问问原因，但自己的英语还不够好。

---

disrespectful *adj.* 无礼的　　　　　　　　　　　interrupt *v.* 中断；打断

be respectful? I wanted to ask her the reason but my English was still not good enough.

I was angry and sad for a few days, until my uncle returned from Taiwan. I asked him, "Why do people get upset simply because I am trying to respect them?" He asked me to tell him the whole story. I told him what happened in school. He told me that what was right back in Taiwan was not necessarily proper here in the United States. He also told me that I should not be sad and that I should try to understand what is done here and *avoid* making the same mistakes.

After the incident, when I'm not sure what to do, I *observe* other people and do things the way they do them. Even though this sometimes makes me feel that I am not being myself, it helps me avoid a lot of cultural difficulties. Of course, now I am also able to ask people questions. As I learn more, life here becomes much more interesting and *enjoyable*.

好几天里我既生气又难过，这时叔叔从台湾回来了。我便问他："为什么因为我想对别人表示尊敬，他们就不高兴呢？"他让我把事情的经过讲给他听。我把在学校的经历说了一遍。他告诉我，在台湾正确的东西现在到了美国就不一定还是正确的了。他还让我不必难过，而应该试着去了解这里人们的行为方式，从而避免再犯同样的错误。

经过这件事后，我再碰到什么自己拿不准的事，就注意观察别人是怎么做的。尽管有时候这样做让我感觉有些失去了自我，但毕竟能帮我避免很多文化上的冲突。当然了，我现在还可以直接开口向别人请教。学到的东西越多，在这儿的生活也就变得更加充满乐趣。

---

avoid *v.* 避免

observe *v.* 观察

enjoyable *adj.* 有趣的；令人愉快的

12

Body Language

My name is Lorena. I was born in Mexico and came to the United States when I was two. *According to* Mexican culture, when spoken to by an adult, children show respect by bowing their heads and not looking the adult directly in the eye. This way of showing respect *caused* me a problem

身体语言

我的名字叫洛蕾娜，出生在墨西哥，两岁的时候来到美国。按照墨西哥文化，小孩子和大人讲话时要低下头，不能直视对方的眼睛，以此来表示尊重。而这种方法让我在学校出了问题。

according to 根据；按照

cause *v.* 引起；导致

when I went to school.

It was a sunny September morning, my first day at my new *private* school. The only person I knew was Tina, a girl from my Sunday school, and we sat next to *each other* and talked. The whole class was talking and giggling; everyone was happy to see old friends again.

Mrs. Georges asked us to be quiet. Then she passed out papers with addition and *subtraction* problems. Almost immediately, Tina asked me, "What did you get for number four?" I started to tell her, but Mrs. Georges called out, "Lorena, turn around and be quiet!" Just then, the school *secretary* came into the room with a message for Mrs. Georges. While they were busy speaking, Tina asked me another question. I turned to tell her to stop. Mrs. Georges must

---

　　那是九月的一天早晨，阳光明媚，我第一天去一间私立学校上学。我只认识一个人，蒂娜，以前周日班上的一个女孩儿。我们坐在一块儿开始聊了起来。满教室都是说话声和笑声，大家见到老朋友都很开心。

　　乔治夫人让我们安静些，然后她分发了试卷，上面是一些加减法的问题。卷子刚发到手，蒂娜就问我："第四题得多少？"我告诉了她。可乔治夫人高声说道："洛蕾娜，转过去，别说话！"就在这时，学校的秘书走进教室，给乔治夫人送来张便条。他们正忙着说话的功夫，蒂娜又问了我一道题。我转过脸去让她别说了。乔治夫人一定看见我的动作了，她喊道："洛蕾娜！马上过来！"

---

private　*adj.* 私有的；私营的；私立的　　　　each other　彼此；互相
subtraction　*n.* 减法　　　　　　　　　　　　secretary　*n.* 秘书

have seen me. She called out, "Lorena, come up here right now!"

My hands got moist. My heart beat fast. I took slow, short steps up to Mrs. Georges's desk. In a whisper I said, "Yes, Mrs. Georges?" I looked down at the floor. Mrs. Georges asked, "What were you doing?" I kept my head down and didn't say anything. Her voice got louder. "What were you doing?"

The next thing I knew, Mrs. Georges *grabbed* my arm tightly. "Look at me when I speak to you!" she said, and she made me look at her. I was *scared* because I had never before looked into the face of an adult who was speaking to me—not even my parents or grandparents.

For the rest of the day I felt very upset, and when I got home, I told my parents what happened. The next day, my mom went to

---

　　我的手心都湿了，心扑通扑通直跳。我慢慢地走到乔治夫人的讲台前。低声说道："是的，乔治夫人？"然后低着头看着地面。乔治夫人问道："你在干什么？"我一直低着头，什么也不说。她的声音抬高了，"你在干什么？"

　　紧接着，乔治夫人紧紧地抓住我的胳膊，"我跟你说话的时候看着我！"她说道，然后就让我看着她。我害怕极了，因为以前和大人说话的时候从来没有看过他们的脸——就连和爸爸妈妈或爷爷奶奶也没有过。

　　那一天我一直闷闷不乐，回到家后把发生的事跟爸爸妈妈讲了。第二天，妈妈和我一起去学校。我们见到了乔治夫人，向她解释说，在我们的

---

grab *v.* 抓住；抓牢　　　　　　　scared *adj.* 害怕的；惊恐的

school with me. We met with Mrs. Georges and explained that in our culture it was disrespectful to look an older person in the eye. Mrs. Georges explained that in American culture it was disrespectful not to look someone in the eye. When I understood, I told Mrs. Georges that I was sorry. She said she was sorry too, and then she gave me a great big hug.

As a result of this experience I always try to look at anyone who is speaking. I'm a part of America because I live here. I have had to *adapt*, and now I tell my own child to look at me when I speak to her. I do not want her to experience what I did. That day in school, Mrs. Georges and I learned something about each other's culture. We learned the hard way, but it helped us both.

文化里，看着长辈的眼睛说话是不尊重的。乔治夫人也告诉我们，在美国文化中不看着对方的眼睛说话是不尊重的表现。我明白了之后，对乔治夫人说对不起，她也表示了歉意，还使劲儿拥抱了我一下。

经过这件事后，我再和别人说话的时候都会尽量看着对方。我也是美国的一部分，因为我就生活在这里，我一定要去适应。现在我也告诉自己的孩子说话的时候要看着我，不想让她再有我那样的经历。那天在学校，乔治夫人和我都对对方的文化有了一些了解，虽然方式不太好，但对我们双方都有帮助。

adapt *v.* 适应；使适合

13

Gestures

My name is Nick. I'm from Canada. In 1998, I was on the island of Pohnpei in the *Pacific Ocean*. I went to teach at a school there. On my first day on the island, something *unusual* happened.

It was very hot, and I was thirsty. I

肢体语言

我叫尼克，是加拿大人。1998年的时候，我在位于太平洋的波纳佩岛上教书。我刚到这座岛屿的第一天就有不同寻常的事情发生了。

当时天气很热，我口渴极了。我走进一家小商店，对柜台后面的女店

Pacific Ocean 太平洋   unusual *adj.* 不寻常的

went into a small store. I spoke to the woman behind the counter. "Do you have any cold drinks?" I asked.

The woman looked at me, but she didn't say anything. I thought she didn't understand me, so I tried easier words, "Do you have Coke?"

Again, the woman was silent. She didn't answer, so I thought that she didn't have any Coke. I spoke louder and more slowly. "Do you have anything else?"

The woman walked over to a *refrigerator*. She opened the door and pointed to many different kinds of *soda*. She didn't say anything, but she removed a Coke and put it on the counter. Speaking slowly

---

主说："你这儿有什么冷饮吗？"

那个女人看了我一眼，但什么也没说。我以为她没听懂我的话，于是便试着用更简单的词问道："你这儿有可乐吗？"

她还不出声，我就以为她这里没有可乐。我提高了嗓音，而且说得更慢一些，"你有别的什么可以喝的吗？"

女店主走到一台冰箱前，打开门，指着里面各种各样的饮料。还是什么也没说，但她却拿出一罐可乐，放在柜台上。我缓慢而清楚地说："多

---

refrigerator n. 冰箱　　　　　　　　　soda n. 汽水；苏打水

and clearly, I asked, "How much does it cost?"

In perfect English, she answered, "Fifty cents."

On Pohnpei, people say yes by raising their *eyebrows* a little. The woman raised her eyebrows when Nick asked questions. Nick did not see her *gesture* because it had no meaning for him. In Canada, raised eyebrows do not answer questions. Canadian people speak or move their heads up and down to say yes.

Later, Nick found out that all of the people on Pohnpei raise their eyebrows to say yes.

少钱？"

"五十美分。"她用标准的英语回答道。

在波纳佩岛，人们轻轻地扬一下眉头，以此来表示肯定的回答。这位女店主在尼克问她问题时就是这样回答的，但尼克没有注意到她的动作，因为对他来说这样没什么含义。在加拿大，动眉头不是用来回答问题的方法，人们用言语或点头来表示肯定回答。

后来，尼克发现波纳佩岛上所有人都是用扬眉来表示"是"的。

---

eyebrow n. 眉毛　　　　　　　　　　gesture n. 姿态；手势

Touching in Public

My name is May, and I came from Taiwan. Back there best friends always walk hand in hand because holding hands is our way of showing *friendship*. Now that I have been here for several years, I know that friends of the same *sex*, and even mothers

公共场合的身体接触

我的名字叫梅，来自中国台湾。在那里，好朋友经常手拉手走在一起，因为牵手是我们表达友谊的一种方式。我在美国生活了几年，了解到同性朋友，甚至母亲和十几岁的女儿之间走路的时候都很少拉手，而我刚来的时候对此一无所知。

friendship *n.* 友谊；友情   sex *n.* 性别

and teenage daughters, seldom go hand in hand, but I didn't know that when I first came to America.

My first year in the United States, I met a girl who had been my classmate in Taiwan. We were excited that we had met again on the other side of the earth, and of course we became best friends. No one really knew about us being best friends because we weren't in the same class. Then one day we were walking hand in hand down the street to get some ice cream. A classmate saw us and seemed very surprised to see us like that. She told us that in the United States, if people walk hand in hand, other people will think they are lovers. Friends usually don't hold hands. After that, we never went hand in hand in public, but only when we were in our own houses or among Chinese people.

A few months later, my *cousin* visited me from Taiwan. She

我刚到美国后的第一年，遇到了一位以前在台湾时的同班同学。能在地球另一端重逢，我们都感到十分高兴，很自然地便成了最要好的朋友。因为我们不在一个班，所以别人并不知道这一点。有一天，我俩手拉着手去街上买冰淇淋。一个同学看到我们的样子，似乎有些惊讶。她说，在美国如果牵手走在一起，别人会以为这两个人是情侣，朋友之间通常不会拉手。从那以后，我俩在公共场合再也不拉手了，只有在自己家里或者和中国人在一起时才会这样。

几个月后，我的表妹从台湾来看我。她很快就注意到我不和她拉着手

---

cousin *n.* 堂兄弟姐妹；表兄弟姐妹

immediately *noticed* that I didn't walk hand in hand with her. She felt sad because she thought I didn't like her as I used to. I tried to explain, but she didn't understand. Finally, a few years later, I went back there for summer *vacation*. When I went out with my family or old friends shopping, to movies, or anywhere else, I walked hand in hand with them. My cousin was so happy that I liked her again. I told her that I always liked her and that I will explain everything to her when she grows up more. After all, it is hard for a person to understand or accept that other places have different cultures if he or she has never lived in a different place.

一起走了。她很难过，因为觉得我不像以前那样喜欢她了。我试着解释，但她并不理解。几年之后，我回台湾过暑假。和家人或者老朋友出去逛街、看电影什么的，我都和他们拉着手走。表妹很开心，我又喜欢她了。我对她说其实我一直都很喜欢她，还告诉她再长大一些我会给她解释这一切。当然，对于没有在别的地方生活过的人来说，确实不太容易理解和接受其他地方不同的文化。

---

notice *v.* 注意　　　　　　　　　　　　　vacation *n.* 假期

15

Dating

I am a Chinese girl from Vietnam, and my name is Nancy. My parents, who are very strict, did not let me *date* until I was eighteen. My first boyfriend was an American *guy* named Ian. Although my parents were opposed to my seeing him, they learned to accept it because they wanted me to be

约会

我是一个来自越南的中国女孩儿，名叫南希。父母对我要求十分严格，直到十八岁才开始让我和男孩子约会。我的第一个男朋友是一位名叫伊恩的美国小伙子。虽然父母反对我和他交往，但还是接受了，因为他们想让我开心。有一天，我请伊恩来家里吃饭，好让父母见见他。不幸的是，那次邀请却导致了我们关系的结束。

date *v.* 约会   guy *n.* 男人；家伙；小伙子

happy. One day I invited Ian over to my house for dinner so that my parents could meet him. Unfortunately, that invitation led to the end of my relationship with Ian.

According to Chinese *custom*, the guy a girl is dating is expected to be her future husband. I have been exposed to the American *concept* that girls can date any guy they want and not have to worry about making *commitments*. Since my parents are very old-fashioned, we sometimes had *arguments* about dating. Because of these arguments, I should have realized what my parents would do when Ian came to my house. But I didn't. And Ian only expected to have a nice relaxing dinner with my family.

按照中国的习惯，女孩儿约会的小伙子就可能是她未来的丈夫。而我了解到的美国式观念则不同，女孩子可以任意约会，而不必考虑做出什么承诺。因为我父母都是老派作风，我们就约会的问题产生过分歧。正是由于有了分歧，我原本应该想到伊恩来我家时父母会怎样做。但我偏偏就没想到，而伊恩也以为只是要和我家人吃一顿美味而又轻松的晚餐呢。

---

custom n. 习惯；风俗　　　　　　concept n. 观念；概念
commitment n. 承诺；保证　　　　argument n. 争论；争吵

This "relaxing" dinner became a *disastrous* dinner when my parents, especially my mom, started asking Ian questions. And I was the one who had to *translate* these questions. They asked him what his future goals were, what his parents' *occupations* were, how many brothers and sisters he had, and even what his educational and financial background was. I was shocked that my parents actually asked those questions, Ian was more than shocked—he was obviously *stunned*. Fortunately, he was very polite and respectful to my parents and suffered through the night. When it was time for Ian to go home, I could tell from the expression on his face that he was glad to be going.

这顿"轻松"的晚餐随着我父母,尤其是我母亲开始问伊恩一些问题时,就变成了一场灾难,而我又不得不翻译这些问题。他们问他将来的目标是什么,父母的职业,有几个兄弟姐妹,甚至问到了教育背景和经济状况。我很吃惊他们会真的问出这些问题来,伊恩就不只是吃惊了——他被彻底问懵了!幸好他很有礼貌,对我父母表现得很尊重,总算熬过了这个晚上。当他要回家的时候,从他脸上的表情可以看出来他有种如释重负的感觉。

---

disastrous *adj.* 灾难性的;极糟糕的
occupation *n.* 职业;工作

translate *v.* 翻译
stunned *adj.* 震惊的

Obviously, Ian noticed that my parents were expecting him to be my future husband. But Ian is an American guy and American guys tend to date a lot before they are ready to *settle down*. He told me that it was the first time he had ever gone to a girlfriend's house for dinner where he had to answer so many questions about himself and his family. We decided that, because of our different cultural backgrounds, we would just be friends from then on. I believe we made the right *decision*.

伊恩显然也注意到我父母是把他当成未来的女婿来看待。但他是个美国男孩儿，他们在准备安定下来之前会和很多女孩子交往。他告诉我说，这还是他头一次去女朋友家吃饭，要回答这么多关于他自己和家人的问题呢。由于各自不同的文化背景，我们认为还是做朋友比较好。我想我们都做出了正确的决定。

settle down 定居；安定下来   decision *n.* 决定；抉择

16

Weddings I

I'm from China, and my name is Su. The problem I will tell about began one day when I was sitting with friends at *lunchtime* talking and laughing. My friend Jan told the rest of us that we were invited to her sister's *wedding*. I was very excited

婚礼（1）

我来自中国，名叫苏。有一天中午，我正和朋友在午饭时间说说笑笑，这时发生了我要讲的故事。我的朋友简告诉我们，想邀请我们去参加她姐姐的婚礼。我当时很激动，因为从来没参加过美国式的婚礼。她姐姐的婚礼就在下个星期举行。

---

lunchtime *n.* 午餐时间   wedding *n.* 婚礼

because I had never been to an American wedding. Her sister's wedding was going to be held the following week.

When school was over, I rushed home so excited that I forgot to take my *algebra* book. I was thinking of what to wear to the wedding. I thought of wearing black and white but then decided that would not be *appropriate* for a wedding. Well, I sat in my room thinking for hours and still I couldn't come up with anything. Then, looking around my room, I noticed something red and thought, why not wear all red to the wedding?

I asked my mother her *opinion* and she told me that red would be a good color, that in China the color red was for good luck. The next day she went shopping with me. We couldn't find anything for several hours. Finally, I found a red suit that I thought was *fabulous*. It was made out of silk; the pants were very baggy, and the blouse

---

放学后，我兴冲冲地跑回家，都忘了带代数课本。我盘算着穿什么衣服去参加婚礼。想过穿黑色或白色；但都觉得不合适。就这样坐在房间里想了几个小时也没什么结果。这时，我环视四周，看到有红色的东西，心里便想，干吗不穿一身红衣服去参加婚礼呢？

我征求了妈妈的意见，她说红色很好，在中国红色代表着吉祥。第二天她陪我去逛街，找了好久都没有找到。最后我发现了一件红色的套装，我觉得漂亮极了。是丝绸做的，裤子很宽松，衬衫像是一件带透明袖子的外套。然后我去买了一双白色的鞋，前面带着可爱的蝴蝶结。

---

algebra *n.* 代数
opinion *n.* 意见；看法

appropriate *adj.* 适当的
fabulous *adj.* 极好的；极妙的

was like a jacket with see-through *sleeves*. Next, I went to buy a pair of shoes. I bought a white pair with cute red bows on the front.

The day of the wedding my friends picked me up so that we could go together to Jan's house. I was the only one who was wearing red. When we got to Jan's house, she greeted us and gave me this funny look, which I didn't like. She seemed mad, but I didn't know why. When she introduced us to her family, her family also gave me this funny look I didn't like. After that, Jan and her family never spoke to me once the whole day. I wanted to cry because everyone kept looking at me like I had done something wrong.

Finally, the wedding was over. I got home and told my mom what happened. The next day, Jan called me and said we couldn't be friends anymore, but she didn't give me a reason. Later on, one of my friends told me that in Jan's *religion* the color red *represents*

婚礼那天，朋友们来接我一起去简家。我是唯一一个穿红色衣服的。到了那里，她来迎接我们，她看我的眼神很奇怪，我不喜欢那种感觉。她好像很生气，但我不知道为什么。她把我们介绍给家里人，她家里人看我也是用那种怪怪的眼神，让我很不舒服。从那之后，她和她家人再也没有对我说过一句话。我真想大哭一场，因为大家看我的样子就像我做错了什么似的。

婚礼终于结束了。我回到家，跟妈妈讲了事情的经过。第二天，简打电话来说我们不能再做朋友了，但她没有说什么原因。后来，一位朋友告诉我，在简信仰的宗教里，红色代表魔鬼。对她和她家人来说，我穿红色

---

sleeve *n.* 袖子　　　　　　　　religion *n.* 宗教；宗教信仰
represent *v.* 代表着；意味着

the *devil*. To Jan and her family my red dress was disrespectful and a sign of bad luck. They thought that by wearing red I was putting the wedding couple in danger. My friend also told me that at most American weddings the red suit would not have been a problem at all. I found all this confusing, but *at least* I finally understood what had happened.

In conclusion, I think that people shouldn't stop being friends or get angry at other people if they do something wrong just because of a cultural misunderstanding. I think people should talk things over before ending their friendship.

的衣服是非常不尊重他们的表现，同时还表示厄运，会给新婚夫妇带来危险。我的朋友还告诉我在大多数美国婚礼上穿红色衣服都没有问题。我觉得这一切都令人费解，但至少让我明白发生了什么事。

我对这件事的总结是，如果别人仅仅因为文化方面的误解而做错事，那不应该和他们断交或生他们的气，绝交之前应该把事情说清楚。

---

devil *n.* 魔鬼；恶魔   at least *至少*
in conclusion *总之；最后*

17

Weddings Ⅱ

My name is Ted. I live near Chicago. I work in an *electronics* store at the mall. A friend works there with me. His name is Mickey and he is Irish-American. I am African-American. My sweetheart, Gail, and I got married. We invited Mickey to the wedding.

婚礼（2）

我叫泰德，住在离芝加哥不远的地方，在一座购物中心里的电器商店工作。我有一个朋友也在那儿上班，他叫米奇，是爱尔兰裔美国人。我本人是一个非裔美国人，我和心爱的女友盖尔刚刚结婚，我们邀请了米奇来参加婚礼。

electronics *n.* 电子器件；电子设备

It was a beautiful wedding. The church was filled with flowers. Gail wore a long white dress. I wore a *tuxedo*. All the guests were in formal clothes too, including Mickey.

After the *minister* said, "You are now husband and wife," we kissed. Then my sister came to the front of the church. She put a *plain* old broom on the floor in front of us. In our formal wedding clothes, Gail and I jumped over the broom. I looked at Mickey. He was trying to be polite, but he looked so surprised. I had to laugh!

那真是一场美丽的婚礼，教堂里布满了鲜花。盖尔穿着长长的白色婚纱，而我则身着燕尾服。所有的宾客也都穿得很正式，其中便有米奇。

在牧师宣布"你们现在结为夫妇"之后，我们深情一吻。然后我姐姐来到教堂前面，她将一把很普通的旧扫帚放在我俩面前的地上。我们穿着正式的礼服，一起从上面跳了过去。我看了米奇一眼，他虽然尽量想表现得有礼貌，但还是一副惊诧不已的样子。我忍不住笑了！

---

tuxedo *n.* 燕尾服；无尾礼服   minister *n.* 牧师
plain *adj.* 简单的；朴素的

Ted and Gail were following an old African-American wedding custom. It goes back to the time of *slavery*. Slaves could not get married in church. Jumping over the broom was a way to marry without a church or a minister. Ted and Gail were honoring their African-American *ancestors*. The broom was from Ted's family. His parents and grandparents jumped over it at their weddings.

Irish-Americans do not have the same custom. Ted knew Mickey would be surprised. He was waiting to see Mickey's face when they jumped over the broom.

泰德和盖尔正在进行的是一项古老的黑人婚礼习俗。这要追溯到奴隶制时代，当时奴隶们不能在教堂里结婚，而跳扫帚就是在没有教堂或牧师的情况下成亲的一种办法。泰德和盖尔以此来表示对自己非洲祖先的敬意。这把扫帚是泰德一家的传家宝，他的父母和祖父母在他们的婚礼上就是从它上面跳过去的。

爱尔兰裔的美国人没有这样的习俗。泰德知道米奇会感到吃惊。他们从扫帚上跳过去的时候，他就等着看米奇脸上惊诧的表情呢。

---

slavery n. 奴隶制度　　　　　　　　　　ancestor n. 始祖；祖先

18

Luck

One summer, I was traveling with my husband, Jon. We were on a crowded bus in Texas. Most of the *passengers* spoke *Spanish*. Suddenly, Jon said, "Natalie, look at those people with the beautiful baby." He pointed to a young

运气

年夏天，我和我的丈夫，强一起去旅游。我们坐在得克萨斯州一辆拥挤的汽车上，很多乘客都说西班牙语。忽然，强说："纳塔莉，看那些人，还有那个漂亮的婴儿。"他指着一个年轻的家庭。他们看上去非常开心。我冲他们微笑了一下，然后用我说得最好的一句西班牙语说："Que chulo!"（"真可爱呀！"）。

---

passenger *n.* 乘客   Spanish *n.* 西班牙语

family. They looked so happy. I smiled at them. Then, in my best Spanish, I said, "Que chulo!" ("How charming!") and *praised* the baby.

Now the parents did not look happy. They looked worried. They got up from their seats and came toward us. When they were close, the father held out the baby to me. He asked me to touch the baby.

The baby's father spoke to Natalie in Spanish. He said that praise from a *stranger* might bring bad luck. The baby could get sick or even die. But if Natalie touched the baby, Natalie was not a stranger anymore. Her praise could not hurt the baby. So the parents wanted Natalie to touch their baby—to protect him from bad luck. Natalie smiled and took the baby. She held him for a minute. The parents smiled too. Now their baby would not have bad luck.

这下子那对父母看上去不那么高兴了，相反却显得很忧虑。他们从座位上站起身朝我们走过来。父亲把孩子抱到我面前，他让我用手摸一摸那个婴儿。

孩子的父亲用西班牙语告诉纳塔莉，来自陌生人的赞美可能会带来厄运，孩子也许会生病，甚至死亡。但是如果纳塔莉用手摸一下那个婴儿，那她就不再是陌生人，她的赞美也就不会伤害婴儿了。所以他们让纳塔莉摸一摸婴儿——来保护他不受厄运的侵扰。纳塔莉笑着把孩子接过来，在怀里抱了一会儿。孩子的父母也笑了。现在他们的孩子不会有麻烦了。

---

praise *v.* 称赞；表扬   stranger *n.* 陌生人

Good Luck and Bad Luck

My name is Debby. I was born in China and lived for many years in Hong Kong. When my family moved to the United States, there were many things that we were not used to. We worked hard to learn and *accept* the American *lifestyle* and culture. Making

好运与厄运

我的名字叫黛比，出生在中国大陆，在香港生活了很长时间。我们家刚来到美国的时候，有很多东西都不适应。我们努力去了解和接受美国的生活方式和文化。对我的爷爷奶奶来说做出变化尤其困

---

accept *v.* 接受   lifestyle *n.* 生活方式；生活习惯

changes was especially difficult for my grandparents. They believe that Chinese people should follow Chinese customs no matter where they are.

Three years ago I met a girl named Reyna. She is Hispanic-American and has lived in the United States all her life. We became good friends almost right away. She taught me how to eat Mexican food, and I taught her how to use chopsticks. She told me about Mexican culture, and I told her about Chinese *celebrations* like the celebration of the full moon. On my sixteenth birthday, I invited Reyna to my house to have dinner with my family. My grandmother had made all of my *favorite* Chinese foods. When Reyna came to the house, she handed me a birthday *gift*. My family liked Reyna very much. We had a very nice dinner together, and after dinner we

难，他们认为中国人无论在哪儿都应该遵从中国的习俗。

三年前，我认识了一个名叫蕾娜的女孩儿，她是西班牙裔，一直都生活在美国。我们很就快成了好朋友。她教我吃墨西哥食物，而我则教她如何用筷子；她给我讲墨西哥的文化，我给她讲中国的节日风俗，例如中秋节。我十六岁生日那天，我请蕾娜来和家人一起吃晚饭。奶奶做了所有我爱吃的中国菜。蕾娜来的时候送给我一份生日礼物。我家人也很喜欢她。我们在一起吃了一顿美食，饭后准备打开礼物。因为急着想知道蕾娜送给

celebration *n.* 庆典；庆祝活动　　　　　　　favorite *adj.* 最喜爱的
gift *n.* 礼物

decided to open my gifts. Since I was eager to know what Reyna gave me, I opened her gift first. It was a black and white clock.

When my grandparents saw the clock, the *expressions* on their faces changed instantly. They became very angry and left the living room. Reyna didn't understand what was happening. I explained that getting a clock as a gift is bad luck, and to Chinese people, black and white *objects* are also bad luck. So, to my grandparents, the gift that Reyna gave me meant double bad luck on my birthday. I also told Reyna that another meaning of a clock is the end of life. After she heard my *explanation* of the meaning of her gift, she felt very bad. She didn't know what to do.

When Reyna left, my grandparents told me that I should not be her friend anymore, since she had wished me death on my birthday.

我什么，于是先把她的打开了，原来是一只黑白色的闹钟。

爷爷奶奶看到这只闹钟，脸色一下变了。他们很生气，离开了客厅。蕾娜不明白发生了什么事。我解释说，对中国人来说收到钟是一种厄运，而且黑色和白色的东西也是不吉利的。因此在爷爷奶奶看来，蕾娜的这件礼物意味着我生日的时候送来双倍的厄运。我还告诉她钟的另一个意思是死亡。她听了我的解释很难过，不知道该如何是好。

蕾娜走后，爷爷奶奶告诉我不要再和她交朋友，因为她在我生日那天

---

expression *n.* 表情；神情
explanation *n.* 说明；解释

object *n.* 物体；实物

I tried to explain that American people do not have that *belief*, but my grandparents wouldn't accept my explanation.

The next day, Reyna came to my house again. My grandparents were very rude to her. She gave me a bright red box and said, "Happy Birthday." I was surprised that she was not angry at the way my grandparents *treated* her. I opened the red box. Inside was a bright red dress. I tried it on, and it looked great on me. I showed it to my grandparents and told them it was from Reyna. They smiled at me and Reyna and told her they liked it very much.

As a result of this incident, I learned that Reyna was very understanding and a great friend to have. *Obviously*, Reyna learned never to give clocks or black and white gifts to Chinese people.

咒我死。我试着解释，说美国人不信这个，可他们听不进去我的话。

第二天，蕾娜又来了我家。爷爷奶奶对她的态度很粗暴。她送给我一个鲜红的盒子，说：“生日快乐！”我很吃惊，我爷爷奶奶这样对她而她却不生气。我打开盒子，里面是一件鲜红的连衣裙。我把它穿上，漂亮极了！我给爷爷奶奶看，告诉他们是蕾娜送的。他们笑着看着我和蕾娜，并告诉她他们非常喜欢这件礼物。

从这件事我了解到，雷娜十分善解人意，是一个很好的朋友。显然她知道了再不要把钟或黑白色的礼物送给中国人。

---

belief *n.* 信仰；信念
obviously *adv.* 明显地；显然地

treat *v.* 对待

MCGRAW-HILL

The Classroom

Call me Henry. I grew up in Vietnam, where we usually don't ask questions or have much contact with teachers. Rarely will students raise their hands. From the day I entered *kindergarten* and all the way through high school, I just listened and took *notes* in class. Each

---

课堂

04 我亨利吧。我在越南长大，在那儿我们不怎么问老师问题，和老师之间的交流也不多，学生们都很少举手。从上幼儿园开始一直到中学，在课堂上我只是听讲，记笔记。每天晚上的任务就是把一天

---

kindergarten n. 幼儿园

note n. 笔记

evening it was my *responsibility* to *memorize* the materials that were presented in class that day. There were no discussions, *debates*, or *challenges* to the teachers' point of view. The teachers were always right because they were the teachers. They knew the stuff better than me.

When I came to the United States the school system surprised me. My classes were hardly ever quiet. One day we had a discussion on the topic of gun control. Everyone participated in it. The class atmosphere was exciting and fun. The arguing went on until the end of the class, and everyone seemed to enjoy it. To my surprise the teacher encouraged the discussion and listened to what the students had to say. This felt very different to me. The teacher was

---

中课堂上老师讲的内容完全记住。没有讨论，没有辩论，也不会对老师的观点提出质疑。老师永远是对的，就因为他们是老师，他们知道的就是比我多。

来到美国之后，这里的教学方式让我大吃一惊。我所在的课堂从来没有安静过。有一天我们讨论枪支控制的话题，所有人都参与进来了。课堂气氛十分活跃而有趣，争论一直持续到下课。让我惊讶的是，老师鼓励学生讨论，并认真听大家的发言。这种方式对我而言非常特别。老师对待学

---

responsibility *n.* 责任；任务　　　　　　memorize *v.* 记住；熟记

debate *n.* 辩论　　　　　　　　　　　　challenge *n.* 怀疑；质疑

treating the students like friends, not like in Vietnam where teachers kept their distance from the students. Hearing the discussion, I learned there were many different opinions on the question of gun control. I also learned that a person who is good at *communicating* can *persuade* other people to change their points of view.

Thinking back on school days in Vietnam, I realized that I wasn't very good at communicating with people because I hadn't had the *practice*. I couldn't even express myself clearly about the *materials* that I learned in Vietnam. Fortunately, during the gun-control discussion, the teacher didn't call on me to state my opinion.

From that day I have been working on expressing my thoughts in a clear manner so that people can understand what I mean.

生就像朋友一样，而不像在越南，老师总是和学生保持一定距离。通过这次辩论，我了解到关于枪支控制有这么多不同的意见，还学会了如果一个人擅长交流，就能说服别人改变看法。

回想起在越南上学时的情形，我意识到自己不善于和别人交流，因为从来没有过这样的经验。甚至以前在越南学过的东西都表达不清楚。幸运的是，在这次关于枪支控制讨论中老师没有叫我发表意见。

从那天起，我一直努力把自己的想法表达清楚，好让别人能明白我的意思。

---

communicate *v.* 交流；沟通
practice *n.* 练习；训练

persuade *v.* 说服；劝说
material *n.* 资料；材料

The Changing Role of Women

I am Jennifer. In my senior year in high school, there were many exciting *activities* like dances, *homecoming* picnics, sports contests against the teachers, and, of course, the *prom*!

女性角色的转变

我叫詹妮弗。高中毕业那年有很多有意思的活动，例如舞会，老生返校野餐会，与老师对抗的体育比赛，当然了，还有毕业舞会！

activity *n.* 活动   homecoming *n.* 校友返校日
prom *n.* 毕业舞会

Prom night was coming, and tickets went on sale. They cost $89 for a couple. Single guys *roamed* the school, looking for girls to ask out. A friend told me that one of his friends wanted to go to the prom with me. Eventually I met the friend, Eddie, and we got along just fine. Gentleman-like, Eddie offered to pay for our prom tickets. However, he *insisted* that I pay for the prom pictures, and trying to do my part, I agreed. At the prom, everything went just great. We danced, ate, and *chatted* for at least five hours.

舞会那晚就要到了，正在售票，每两张票89美元。单身男孩在校园里转来转去，寻找自己想邀请的女孩。一个朋友跟我说，他有个朋友想邀请我一起参加舞会。后来我看到了这位名叫艾迪的朋友，我们相处得不错。他很绅士，提出由他来付舞会的门票，但坚持由我来付舞会照片的钱。为了礼尚往来，我便同意了。舞会上一切都很好，我们跳舞、吃东西、聊天，玩了至少五个小时。

---

roam *v.* 漫步；闲逛　　　　　　　　　　　　　　　insist *v.* 坚持
chat *v.* 聊天

After the prom, we went to a *restaurant* and had dinner. The dinner was great, too, but when it was over, the trouble began. Eddie just sat there, even though he had finished eating. Thinking that he was tired, I just sat there too. Then it turned out that Eddie expected me to pay for the meal. I was *horrified* because, according to Chinese customs, a guy always pays for everything when he asks a girl out. I was already surprised when Eddie had insisted that I pay for the prom pictures, but this was too much for me. Eventually I paid and Eddie drove me home. I did not talk to him for a very long time. Later on, I found out that there is an American custom of "splitting the bill," where each *individual* pays half. It took me a long time to *adapt* to this custom!

舞会结束后，我们去一家餐厅吃晚饭。那顿饭也很棒，但到结束的时候，麻烦来了。尽管已经吃完了，但艾迪还是坐在那儿不动。我还以为他太累了呢，于是也没动。后来才发现艾迪在等我付账。按照中国的传统，当男孩约女孩出来时他应为所有花销付款，他坚持我付舞会照片的钱我已经很吃惊了，但这样真是太过分了！最后我付了钱，艾迪开车送我回家。我很长时间没跟他说话。后来我才发现有"分开付账"这样一个美国式的习惯，每人各付一半。我花了好长时间才适应了这种做法！

---

restaurant *n.* 餐馆
individual *n.* 个人；个体

horrify *v.* 使震惊
adapt *v.* 适应

22

Age

My name is Patchara. Fifteen years ago, I moved to the United States from *Thailand*. I work as a *waitress* in a restaurant. An older man and woman come in for dinner once a week. They are very nice. When they enter, I say,

---

年龄

我叫帕查拉，十五年前从泰国移民来美国，现在在一家餐厅做服务员。有一对老年夫妇每星期来我们店里用一次餐，他们人很好，很和蔼。他们进门的时候，我说："您好，爸爸！您好，妈妈！"然后双掌合十，鞠上一躬。在泰国我们就是这样和老年人打招呼，以表示尊

Thailand *n.* 泰国   waitress *n.* 女服务员

"Hello, Papa. Hello, Mama. " Then I put my hands together and *bow*. That is how we greet older people in Thailand. It shows respect. But this couple doesn't like it. Now, when they come in, they don't want to sit in my area. They want a different waitress to serve them.

Patchara embarrassed the couple. She drew *attention* to their age. These customers feel young. They don't want to think they look old. In fact, they are not young. Last year, their children gave them a party to celebrate their fiftieth wedding *anniversary*. They are proud of their long marriage and proud of their grandchildren, but they don't want to think about their age. Many Americans are not happy to get old.

重。但这对老夫妇却不喜欢这一做法，现在他们来的时候不想坐在我服务的区域里了，而是要别人为他们服务。

帕查拉使这对老夫妇感到有些尴尬，她让别人注意到他们的年龄。两位老人自我感觉很年轻，不愿想起自己的老态。实际上他们已经不年轻了，去年孩子们为这对老夫妇举办了结婚五十周年纪念庆典，他们为自己长久的婚姻和一群孙子孙女感到骄傲，但却不愿意去想自己的年龄。很多美国人都不喜欢变老。

---

bow *v.* 鞠躬　　　　　　　attention *n.* 注意力；关注
anniversary *n.* 周年纪念日

Attitudes Toward Aging

When my family *emigrated* from a small village in Canton, China, we brought not only our *luggage*, but also our village's rules, customs, and *superstitions*. One of the rules is that youngsters should always respect elders. Unfortunately, this rule resulted in my very first embarrassment in the United States.

对待年老的态度

当我们家从中国广东的一座小村庄移民到美国时，随之带来的不仅是行李，还有我们村的规矩、习俗和迷信。其中一条规矩便是：年轻人要尊重年长者。不幸的是，这条规矩却导致了我到美国后第一件尴尬的事。

emigrate *v.* 移民   luggage *n.* 行李
superstition *n.* 迷信

I had a *part-time* job as a waiter in a Chinese restaurant. One time, when I was serving food to a middle-aged couple, the wife asked me how the food could be served so quickly. I told her that I had made sure they got their food quickly because I always respect the elderly. As soon as I said that, her face showed great *displeasure*. My manager, who had *overheard*, took me aside and gave me a long *lecture* about how sensitive Americans are and how they dislike the description "old". I then walked back to the table and apologized to the wife. After the couple listened to my explanation, they understood that the incident was caused by cultural differences, so they laughed and were no longer angry.

In my village in China, people are proud of being old. Not that many people survive to the age of fifty or sixty, and people who reach such an age have the most knowledge and experience.

我在一家中餐馆兼职做服务生。一次我在为一对中年夫妇服务的时候，那位妻子问我菜怎么会上得这么快。我告诉她尽量快上是因为我尊重老人。话音刚落，她的脸色立刻变得很难看。经理在旁边听到了，把我领到一边，讲了一大通美国人是如何敏感，还有他们多么不喜欢"老"这个词。然后我回到了桌旁，向那位妻子道歉。这对夫妇听了我的解释后，明白这件事是由文化差异引起的，于是笑了起来，不再生气了。

在我们村子里，人们以年长为骄傲，不仅是因为活到五六十岁，而是因为活到这个年龄之后就会拥有更多的人生阅历。年轻人对老人都非常尊

---

part-time *adj.* 兼职的

overhear *v.* 无意中听到

displeasure *n.* 不愉快；不满；生气

lecture *n.* 讲话；教训

Youngsters always respect older people because they know they can learn from this valuable experience.

However, in the United States aging is considered a problem since "old" means that a person is going to *retire* or that the body is not functioning so well. Here many people try to *avoid* old age by doing exercises or jogging, and women put on makeup hoping to look young. When I told the couple in the restaurant that I respect the elderly, they got angry because this made them feel they had failed to *retain* their youth. I had told them something they didn't want to hear.

As a result of this experience, I have changed the way I am with older people. This does not mean that I don't respect them anymore; I still respect them, but now I don't *express* my feelings through words.

敬，因为能从他们那里学到有价值的经验。

然而在美国，年龄的增长却被认为是问题，因为"老"意味着人要退休，或是身体机能不如从前了。这里的很多人通过做运动或慢跑来延缓衰老，妇女使用化妆品以显得年轻。当我对餐厅那对夫妇说自己尊敬老人时，他们很生气是因为这让他们感觉到没能够保持住青春，我说了一些他们不想听到的话。

这件事发生后，我改变了与老年人交往的方法。这并不意味着不再尊重他们，我对他们尊敬的心情不会变，但现在不再用话语表达自己的感情了。

---

retire *v.* 退休　　　　　　　　avoid *v.* 避免；防止
retain *v.* 保持；保留　　　　　express *v.* 表达

Stereotypes and Prejudice

sticks & stones

My name is Teresa. My parents are from Mexico but moved to the United States, where I was born. When I was twelve years old I was bused from my neighborhood to a community nearby for junior high school. My *reaction* when I got to the school was one of culture shock. The *majority* of students, teachers, and staff were Anglo. I had never been in such an *environment* before. Up to then I

成见与偏见

我的名字叫特雷莎，父母都是墨西哥人，他们移民来到美国，我就出生在这里。十二岁那年，我每天坐校车去另外一个居民区上初中。我到那所学校后的反应就是一种文化冲击。大部分学生、教师和工作人员都是白人。在这之前我从未在这样的环境中生活过，一直都是在

reaction *n.* 反应　　　　　　　majority *n.* 多数；大部分
environment *n.* 生活环境

MCGRAW-HILL

had been in a completely Hispanic neighborhood and school. The first thing that ran through my head was, where have I been?

I felt as if I was in another world of people who looked different, acted differently, spoke and dressed differently. I didn't know how to *behave* or what to say. They wore what I later discovered to be *designer jeans* and backpacks. They also seemed to be wealthy, because they paid cash for their meals while I used reduced meal tickets.

I didn't have any friends at first. I didn't know any of the students who rode the bus with me, and in most of my classes I was the only Hispanic. I was shy and embarrassed. I felt very *intimidated* by all

---

西班牙裔的居民区生活、读书。我脑海里出现的第一个念头就是，我这是到哪儿了？

我感觉自己像是到了另一个世界，人们的长相、穿衣打扮、言谈举止都是那么不同。我不知道该怎么做，该说什么。他们穿的戴的我后来才知道原来叫名牌牛仔裤和双肩背包。他们好像很有钱，因为都用现金买东西吃，而我用的是饭票。

刚开始的时候我没有什么朋友，那些和我一起坐校车的学生都不认识，而且在很多课堂里我都是唯一的西班牙裔。我感到很害羞，很难为

---

behave *v.* 表现
jeans *n.* 牛仔裤
designer *adj.* 由著名设计师设计的
intimidated *adj.* 胆怯的；怯场的

these very verbal and confident *individuals*. I also felt vibrations of hate and *resentment* from these people, although I wasn't sure why. I had no one to talk to or turn to for help who I thought would be able to understand. I had no Hispanic role *models*.

During the first week of school, there was an incident. As my bus was leaving the school, a bunch of Anglo kids began throwing eggs at the bus and screaming, "Go home, beaners!" I had no idea what a "beaner" was or why the kids would be so *cruel*. This incident stayed with me. I earned A's in most of my classes. As time went on, I became friends with other Hispanics and with Anglo kids. But I

情，和那些侃侃而谈而又充满自信的人在一起我心里总是有种恐惧感。同时也能感受到来自他们的厌恶和憎恨，尽管不明白是为什么。我没有朋友可以说话，也没有人能理解我，帮助我。周围没有可以让我效仿的西班牙裔人做榜样。

开学后第一周发生了一件事。当时校车刚离开学校，一群白人孩子开始朝校车扔鸡蛋，并喊着："回家去吧！黑豆！"我不明白"黑豆"是什么意思，也不理解这些孩子为什么那么粗暴。这件事一直困扰着我。我的大多数科目都拿了A，同时随着时间的推移也交了一些西班牙裔和白人朋

---

individual *n.* 个人

model *n.* 模范；典型；榜样

resentment *n.* 愤恨；怨恨

cruel *adj.* 残暴的；残酷的

still felt hurt, mad, and a little confused. Deep inside I knew that the majority of the Anglo kids did not want any "beaners" in their school. They must have felt invaded, and I think that since they did not really know many Hispanics, they probably had hundreds of *stereotypes* about us.

How did I feel at the end of my first year? I felt that my experience had been very *meaningful* and *educational*. I was amazed by how much I had learned about another part of society. My *attitudes* toward these "other" people had changed greatly. Above all, I felt that my eyes had been opened to more of what life had to offer and that I had learned quite a lot academically, probably more than I would have learned if I had gone to junior high school in my neighborhood.

友。但我还是感觉很受伤，很生气，还有些迷惑。在内心深处，我知道大多数白人孩子不希望学校里有"黑豆"。他们一定有种被入侵的感觉，而且我想由于他们不认识多少西班牙裔人，所以很可能对我们有很多成见。

读完第一年后我的感觉如何？我认为那段经历非常有意义，富有教育性。我惊讶于自己对社会的另一部分有了如此多的了解，我对"别人"的态度有了巨大的转变。最重要的是，我看待生活的视野开阔了许多，而且学业上进步很大，而当初要是在自己家附近读中学的话，可能就没有这么多收获了。

---

stereotype *n.* 模式化形象；刻板印象
educational *adj.* 有教育意义的

meaningful *adj.* 有意义的
attitude *n.* 态度；看法

Religious Practices **a**nd **B**eliefs

Icame from Mexico, and my name is Amalia. Like most people, my family came to the United States for better *opportunities* in *employment* and education. Learning a new language wasn't easy, and what was even more difficult was learning to live with people from different cultures—not just the American culture, but many

宗教与信仰

我来自墨西哥，名字叫阿玛丽亚。和许多人一样，我的家人来到美国也是为了寻找更好的就业和受教育的机会。学习一门新的语言并不容易，而更难的是学会和来自不同文化的人们一起生活——不仅是美国文化，还有许多不同的文化。我有一次令人尴尬的经历，和我最好

---

opportunity *n.* 机会   employment *n.* 职业；工作

other cultures, too. One of the embarrassing experiences I have had involved my best friend Silvia, who is from Venezuela and is a *Jehovah*'s Witness.

When Silvia told me she was a Jehovah's Witness, I didn't know what that meant. She explained it was a religion. On her sixteenth birthday, Silvia invited me to her house. I was really excited. I thought there would be a party, so the day before I bought Silvia a *present*. It was an *antique* music box. When my dad dropped me off at her house I was surprised because the house seemed lonely and silent. I knocked at the door, and her mom answered. She *greeted* me with a kiss on the cheek and a hug. Then she invited me in. As I entered the living room, I saw a group of people. I greeted them and sat down. A

的朋友西尔维亚有关。她来自委内瑞拉，是一位耶和华见证人会的信徒。

当西尔维亚告诉我她是耶和华见证人会教徒时，我并不明白那是什么意思。她解释说那是一种宗教。她十六岁生日那天，西尔维亚邀请我去她家。我很高兴，以为会有一场晚会呢。前一天我给她买了份礼物，一只古董式音乐盒。当爸爸把我送到她家门口时，我惊讶地发现房子里好像很安静。我敲敲门，她妈妈来开的门，她亲了我脸颊，还拥抱了一下，迎我进了屋。我走进客厅，看到一群人。我和他们打声招呼便坐了下来。不一会儿，西尔维亚

Jehovah *n.* 耶和华（《〈圣经〉旧约》中对上帝的称呼）　　present *n.* 礼物

antique *adj.* 古老的；古董的　　greet *v.* 迎接；欢迎

few seconds later, Silvia came downstairs. As she greeted me with a hug and a kiss, I took out the present and said, "Happy Birthday!"

All of a sudden the people in the room stopped talking and stared at Silvia and me. I looked at Silvia with a *puzzled* look. She was just looking down at the ground with a face as red as a tomato. After a few minutes of silence, she said, "I'm sorry, but I can't accept your present. It was really sweet of you." I froze. I was embarrassed, hurt, and *humiliated*. Tears rolled down my *cheeks*. I didn't know what to do. Here I was in the middle of the room with all those people looking at me and not saying anything. I wished they would at least *laugh at* me or something.

After a few minutes I came to reality and ran out of the room. I ran all the way to the driveway. Silvia came running after me. Then

走下楼来。我们拥抱并亲吻，然后我拿出礼物，说："生日快乐！"

屋子里的人一下子全都不出声了，盯着西尔维亚和我看。我疑惑地看着西尔维亚，她眼睛看着地上，脸红得像番茄一样。沉默了一会儿，她说："对不起，我不能接受你的礼物。你真是太好了。"我顿时愣住了，觉得既难堪又委屈，眼泪顺着脸颊流了下来，不知该如何是好。我就那样站在中间，大家都看着我，一言不发。真希望他们哪怕是笑话我或怎么样都会好一些。

过了几分钟，我缓过神来，跑出了屋子，一直跑到车道。西尔维亚随后也跟着跑出来。她解释说，在她的宗教里，人们不庆祝生日，也不庆祝

puzzled *adj.* 困惑的
cheek *n.* 面颊；脸颊

humiliate *v.* 使蒙羞；使出丑
laugh at 嘲笑

she explained that in her religion, they did not *celebrate* birthdays or holidays of any kind, and that the people in her living room were members of her *congregation*. She couldn't accept the present. It would have gotten her in trouble because it was like breaking the law. As I turned to look at her, I saw there were tears in her eyes. "So, I have to keep the present?" I asked. Sadly, she nodded yes, but she gave me a hug and I felt a little better.

As a result of this experience, I've learned not to make *assumptions*. Not everybody has the same *traditions* as I do. Now when I hear of a new religion I ask for information and make sure I don't have another misunderstanding.

任何节日。客厅里那些人都是这个教派的会众。她不能接受这份礼物，那样就像触犯法律一样，会给她带来麻烦。我转过身去，看见她眼里含着泪水。"那么，这礼物我得自己留着了？"我问道。她很难过地点点头，但她拥抱了我一下，让我感觉稍微好一些。

从这次经历我得到一个教训，不要随意作任何假设。不是每个人都和我有一样的传统。现在每当我听说一种新的宗教，就去会了解情况，确保不再闹出误会来。

---

celebrate *v.* 庆祝　　　　　　　　congregation *n.* 教堂会众
assumption *n.* 假设；假定　　　　tradition *n.* 惯例；传统

26

Religious Customs

My name is Fay, and I live in New York City. One Friday last January, I had a strange experience. It was late when I left work. It was very cold. I walked from the bus to my *apartment* and saw my new *neighbor*, Shoshana. She was standing outside our apartment building. She stopped a woman and asked her something. The woman looked at Shoshana, shook her head, and walked away. Shoshana stopped the next

宗教习俗

我的名字叫费伊，住在纽约。去年一月的一个星期五，我经历了一件奇怪的事。当时我刚下班，已经很晚了，而且很冷。我从公共汽车站朝公寓走，这时看见了新搬来的邻居，肖珊娜。她站在公寓门外，拦住一个过路的妇女，对她说了些什么。那个女人看了看肖珊娜，摇摇头，走了。肖珊娜又拦住了一个男人，那人点点头，随她走进了大楼。

apartment *n.* 公寓   neighbor *n.* 邻居

person, a man. He nodded and followed her inside the building. I was worried, so I went to her apartment and knocked on her door.

"Shoshana, it's me, Fay. Is everything all right?"

Shoshana came to the door and invited me in. The man from the street stood next to Shoshana's electric heater. He turned it on.

Shoshana is an *Orthodox Jew*. Her religion says that she cannot do any work on the *Sabbath*. The rule is very strict. She cannot even turn things on and off. But it is all right if a non-Jew does it for her.

The Sabbath begins at *sunset* on Friday. Shoshana got home too late to turn on the heater before sunset. It was very cold. That is why she stopped people on the street. The man who stopped was not Jewish. He often helped his Jewish neighbors. He turned off *air conditioners*, lights, and stoves for them. He was happy to help his Jewish neighbors on their Sabbath.

我很纳闷，于是来到她的房门前，敲了敲门。

"肖珊娜，是我，费伊，没什么事吧？"

肖珊娜开了门，请我进去，街上那个男人站在电暖气前面，伸手把它打开。

肖珊娜是一位正统犹太教信徒，她所信奉的宗教规定在安息日那天不能做任何工作。这条规定非常严格，她甚至不能开关电器。但如果有一个非犹太教徒帮她做就没问题了。

安息日从周五的日落时开始，肖珊娜回来很晚，没法在天黑之前把暖气打开，而天气又非常冷。于是她就去街上找人帮忙。那个男人不是犹太教徒，他经常帮自己的犹太人邻居做些事情，如关空调、电灯和炉子等等，他也很愿意在安息日里帮助他们。

Orthodox Jew 正统的犹太教信徒   Sabbath *n.* 安息日

sunset *n.* 日落；傍晚   air conditioner 空调设备；空调机

27

Health and Illness

My father was born in China, and my mother was born in Cambodia. They *adopted* the *traditional* values of their cultures and passed these values on to me. I was also born in Cambodia, but my family and I have been living in the United States for about ten years now. I have even chosen an American name and call myself Wendy.

健康与疾病

我的父亲是中国人，母亲是柬埔寨人。他们接受了各自文化中的传统价值观念，并把它们传给了我。我本人也出生在柬埔寨，但现在已经和家人在美国生活近十年了。我还起了一个美国式的名字，叫温迪。

---

adopt *v.* 采用；采纳

traditional *adj.* 传统的

There were not many Asian students where I first went to school, so when I got sick I didn't know what to do, whether to stay home or go to school. One day when I got home I didn't feel well. My mother felt my *forehead* and noticed that I *had a fever*. She said, "I'd better coin you to *get rid of* the bad pressure so you can go to school tomorrow."

Coining is a Cambodian tradition we use to help us feel better when we are sick. A coin is dipped in oil and then its edge is *rubbed* against the sick person's chest, back, and neck. Coining hurts. This time it hurt so much that my mother had to put her leg on my back so I would stay still. In the end, I felt better inside, but outside I hurt because of the red lines that appeared from the coining.

刚上学的时候，周围没有多少亚洲学生。所以每次生病的时候都不知该怎么办好，是在家休息还是去上学。有一天回到家里，感觉不是很舒服，妈妈摸了摸我的额头，发现我有些发烧。她说："我最好给你刮痧，把火排出去，这样明天就能上学了。"

刮痧是柬埔寨的一种传统治疗方法，用一枚硬币沾上油，然后用边缘摩擦病人的胸口、后背和脖子。刮痧很疼的，这一次疼得尤其厉害，妈妈得用腿顶住我的后背才能让我不动。弄完之后，我身体感觉好些了，但外面由于刮痧时留下的红线疼得实在难受。

---

forehead *n.* 额；前额   have a fever 发烧

get rid of 摆脱；除去   rub *v.* 擦；摩擦

The next day in class when I went up to ask my teacher about my workbook, she noticed the red marks on my neck and asked me what happened. I tried to explain to her with body language because I couldn't speak well yet. She called someone to take me to the nurse to be examined. The nurse had never seen anything like this before. The *principal* and the nurse showed me all kinds of objects they thought my parents used to *punish* me. They thought I was the *victim* of child abuse. I tried to show them what happened by taking a coin and rubbing it against my arm. They still didn't understand because each red mark was the size of a ruler in width and the marks were deep red like *bruises*.

第二天上课的时候，我站起来问老师作业的事，她注意到我脖子上的红印，便问我是怎么回事。我试着用手势来跟她解释，但没办法说清楚。她叫人把我带到医务室让护士检查，护士从来没见过这种情况。校长和护士找来各种东西让我看，他们以为我父母就是用某种东西来对我进行体罚的，以为我是家庭暴力的牺牲品。我用一枚硬币在胳膊上蹭，试着向他们解释，他们还是没办法明白，因为每道红印都像格尺那么宽，都像瘀血一般深红。

---

principal *n.* 校长   punish *v.* 惩罚
victim *n.* 受害者；牺牲品   bruise *n.* 瘀伤；青肿

The school didn't have an Asian *translator*. I had never been in a *situation* like this, and I was afraid of what the people at school would do to me. But they let me call home and I told my parents what happened. Since my parents couldn't speak English, the school called a church agency, which found a Mandarin translator for us.

The translator and my dad went to the school. The people at the school office had angry faces. All my dad could do was to explain in detail that coining is a part of our tradition and that we were newcomers. The principal was going to report it to the police, but when he finally understood better what had happened, he dropped the case. He advised my parents not to do coining again. He said that next time I was sick I should stay home and go to a doctor for medicine.

学校里没有来自亚洲的翻译，我以前从来没经历过这样的事，所以心里很害怕。他们让我往家里打电话，我把情况跟父母讲了。因为他们不会说英语，于是学校给一家教会组织打电话，找来了一位会说汉语普通话的翻译。

那位翻译和我父亲来到学校，办公室的人都怒气满面。爸爸详细地解释了刮痧是我们传统的一部分，并说明我们是新来到这里的。校长本来打算报警，但当他最终了解情况之后就打消了念头。他建议我父母以后不要再采取刮痧疗法了，他说下次我再生病的话，应该待在家里休息，并去看医生。

---

translator *n.* 译者；翻译

situation *n.* 情况；形势

28

Holidays

Hi. My name is Tony, and I remember the first *Halloween* I spent in the United States. I was in the sixth grade, trying my best to study as hard as I could to *overcome* the language *barrier*. Even though I studied English in my hometown, Hong Kong, I was still not able to communicate in English. I realized

节日

嗨！我叫托尼，直到今天我还记得第一次在美国过万圣节前夜时的情形。那时我正上六年级，拼命地学习以克服语言障碍。尽管在香港的时候也学过，但还是无法用英语进行交流。那天我听到同学们

Halloween *n.* 万圣节前夕　　　　　　　　　　overcome *v.* 克服
barrier *n.* 障碍；阻碍

that my classmates were talking about how they would dress on Halloween, but I didn't know what Halloween was.

That year Halloween came on Saturday. I was home most of the day studying. I didn't have a chance to go outside and see how everyone was dressed, because if I had, the following incident would not have happened.

After dinner, my parents *turned off* all the lights and went to their room. They did this so they could *ignore* the children coming to the house for treats. But they didn't tell me about it. I was in my room, so I didn't know what was happening. After a while I went out of my room to get a drink of water. I realized that the house was dark very early, and I thought that my parents were tired after a long day of work. I didn't have any brothers or sisters to come with me, so I felt very much alone in the dark house. I was not used to that. Then it

---

在议论万圣节前夜穿什么服装，但并不明白那究竟是什么意思。

那年的万圣节前夜恰好是星期六。白天大部分时间我都在家里学习，没有机会去外边看别人穿什么衣服。如果当时看到的话，那接下来的事就不会发生了。

吃完晚饭后，爸爸妈妈把灯关掉，回他们的房间去，这样一来就不用去管那些来要东西的孩子了。但是他们没有把这件事告诉我，我也就不知道出了什么事。过了一会儿，我从自己的房间里出来找水喝，发现房子里黑得比平时早，还以为是爸爸妈妈工作了一天太疲倦了。我没有兄弟姐

---

turn off 关掉；关闭   ignore v. 忽视；不顾

happened. When I was drinking my glass of water, the *doorbell* rang. I looked out of my window. There, standing at my front door, were four or five *ghosts* accompanied by a *witch*!

I was so scared that I started screaming and I covered myself with my *blanket*. I tried not to scream, but I couldn't stop. My father came running into my room asking me what was the matter. I told him about the ghosts and the witch, and he explained to me about Halloween. I was relieved after realizing the truth but I also felt embarrassed about being afraid.

That was my first experience with Halloween. Now, each year I remind my parents, weeks before Halloween, to buy candy, and when I do, my dad laughs at me about that incident.

妹，所以在黑洞洞的房子里感到非常孤单，很不习惯。就在这时发生了一件事。我正喝水呢，忽然门铃响了。我从窗户向外看去，就在那儿，在我家门口，站着四五个鬼怪，还有个女巫！

我吓坏了，大声尖叫起来，并用毯子把自己蒙上。我也不想喊，但是控制不住。爸爸跑进来，问出什么事了。我跟他说有鬼和女巫。他给我讲了万圣节前夜是怎么回事。我了解真相后才放心了。但是因为自己害怕而感到有些难为情。

那是我第一次经历万圣节前夜。现在每年快到那一天时，我都会提醒父母买些糖果准备着，而爸爸就会拿那件事来笑话我一下。

doorbell *n.* 门铃　　　　　　ghost *n.* 鬼；幽灵
witch *n.* 巫婆；女巫　　　　　blanket *n.* 毛毯；毯子

The New Year

My name is Mrs. Buranen. I teach seventh grade in the United States. Usually my students behave very well—they almost never make trouble. But one April day some of my students were very excited and noisy. In the hall and on the playground, these students threw cups of water at *each other*. They even threw

---

新年

我的名字是布拉南夫人，在美国教七年级。通常来说我的学生们表现都很好——他们几乎从不惹什么麻烦。但是，四月份的一天，我的一些学生忽然变得非常兴奋，并且大声喧闹。他们在走廊里和操场上用杯子互相往身上泼水。甚至还朝我和我的助教身上泼！

---

each other 彼此；互相

water at my teacher's *aide* and me!

I told the students to stop, but they continued their game. My teacher's aide didn't help me. She watched the students and smiled. Finally I got angry. I began to *scold* the noisy students, but my teacher's aide said, "Wait!"

The date was April 13. The teacher's aide told Mrs. Buranen that it was the Cambodian New Year. The aide knew this because she was from Cambodia. The students who threw the water were Cambodian, too. It is a Cambodian custom to throw water at others on New Year's Day. Cambodians believe that it brings good luck and happiness all year. Sometimes they color the water red, pink, or yellow to show their hopes for a happy future. The students threw water at Mrs. Buranen to wish her good luck for the new year.

　　我让学生们停下来，但他们却毫不理会，仍旧在那里玩闹。我的助教也不帮我，她只是微笑着看着他们。我最后真的生气了！我开始斥责那些大声喧闹的学生，但我的助教却说："等一等！"

　　这一天是4月13日，助教告诉布拉南夫人，这是柬埔寨的新年。她了解这一点是因为她本人就是柬埔寨人。而那些泼水玩儿的学生们也来自柬埔寨。在新年那一天互相往身上泼水是柬埔寨人的一个习俗，他们认为这样会带来一年的吉祥和幸福。有的时候他们还把水染成红、粉或黄等各种颜色，来表达对美好未来的期盼。这些学生朝布拉南夫人身上泼水就是在向她表示新年的祝福。

---

aide *n.* 助手　　　　　　　　　　　　scold *v.* 责骂；训斥

Parents and Children

My name is Lily, and I was raised in a very *conservative* family on the *island* of Fiji, in the South Pacific. At an early age we were taught close family ties and conservative ways. Family members worked together as one unit, and we respected our elders. Upon arriving in the United States, I discovered a very different

父母与子女

我的名字叫莉莉，来自南太平洋上的斐济岛，从小在一个传统式家庭里长大。很小的时候父母便灌输给我紧密的家庭纽带观念和传统的生活方式。家庭成员要作为一个整体共同努力，我们要尊敬长辈。自从来到美国，我发现了一个截然不同的世界，这里的孩子随心所欲

---

conservative *adj.* 保守的；守旧的；传统的　　　　　island *n.* 岛；岛屿

world, where children speak as they wish to their parents and at times even treat them with *disrespect*. This different world eventually led to some difficulties between me and my parents.

When I was eighteen, a couple of my friends moved out of their parents' house and into an apartment of their own. They asked me to move in with them. These friends were born in the United States, and their *upbringing* was less conservative than mine. Their parents *considered* it perfectly *acceptable* for them to move out and live independently at eighteen. But when I spoke to my parents, it was clear they did not want me to leave home. My friends couldn't understand this and they kept telling me to move out anyway. I felt caught between my friends and my parents. I felt that my friends were doing something that was socially acceptable and "in with the crowd" and that my parents were being old-fashioned and not behaving as Americans should behave.

地对父母说出自己的想法，有时甚至对待父母不是很尊重。这个不同的世界最终导致我和父母之间出现了一些问题。

　　我十八岁那年，几个朋友从父母家里搬出来，住进了自己的公寓。他们想让我也一起去住。这些朋友都出生在美国，所受的教育不像我那样传统。他们的父母认为，到了十八岁自己出去独立生活是完全可以接受的。可当我和父母说了之后，很明显他们不愿意让我离开家。而朋友们对此并不理解，还继续催促我搬出去。我感觉自己被夹在了朋友和父母中间，觉得朋友的行为是为社会所接受的，是很合群的；而父母则太过老套，行为方式不够美国化。

---

disrespect　*n.* 无礼；不尊敬
consider　*v.* 认为；看待

upbringing　*n.* 教养；养育
acceptable　*adj.* 可接受的

For me, after many *sleepless* nights, my *obligation* as a daughter *overcame* my yearning for independence. I realized that my parents' *unwillingness* for me to move out was because of their love for me. I also realized that if my friends were true friends they would accept my decision. I told them I'd decided to stay with my parents. Some of my friends and I grew apart from each other but most of my friends accepted my decision. They realized that it did not matter whether I lived with my parents, that what really mattered for our friendship was how I was with them. Now, looking back, I feel that an eighteen-year-old is still young enough to make many mistakes, and I feel lucky that I didn't make a mistake.

经过许多个不眠之夜后，作为一个女儿的责任感压倒了对于独立的渴望。我明白父母不愿我走是源于他们对我的爱。而且如果我的朋友是真正的朋友，那他们就会接受我的决定。我告诉他们我要留下来和父母一起住。有的人和我疏远了，但大多数都接受了我的决定。他们知道对我们之间的友谊来说，是否和父母住在一起并不重要，重要的是我本人如何与他们相处。现在回过头来看，我感觉十八岁还是太年轻，容易犯许多错误。我很庆幸当时没有做错。

---

sleepless *adj.* 失眠的   obligation *n.* 义务；责任
overcome *v.* 克服；战胜   unwillingness *n.* 不愿意；不情愿

31

Taking Care of Children

My name is Oskar, and I am from *Denmark*. Last year, I had a shocking experience. I visited New York City with my daughter, Kirsten. She was fourteen months old. One day, I put Kirsten in her *stroller* and went to a bank. I wanted to change some money. When we got to the bank, Kirsten was asleep. I went into the bank and left Kirsten outside. I waited in line.

照顾孩子

我的名字叫奥斯卡，来自丹麦。去年我经历了一场不同寻常的事情。我带着我的女儿克里斯汀去纽约游玩，当时她只有十四个月大。一天，我把她放进婴儿车，去一家银行准备换些钱。我们到银行的时候，克里斯汀睡着了。我走进银行，把她留在外面。我站在那儿排队，忽然两个警察走进来把我逮捕了！

Denmark *n.* 丹麦

stroller *n.* 婴儿手推车

Suddenly, two police officers entered the bank. They *arrested* me!

Kirsten *woke up* and began to cry. People worried about her. Two people went into the bank to *look for* Kirsten's parents. They told Oskar that Kirsten was crying, but Oskar did not bring the baby inside. The people called the police. In New York City, parents cannot leave a small child alone. It is *against* the law.

But Oskar said that in Denmark, parents often leave their children outside in strollers. The children are safe. Nobody hurts them. Danish people watch out for each other's children. Oskar thought that things were the same in the United States.

After two days, the police learned that Oskar told them the truth. In Denmark, people really do leave their children alone. The police let Oskar go. He went back to Denmark with Kirsten.

克里斯汀醒来后便哭了起来，周围的人很担心。两个人走进银行找她的父母。他们告诉奥斯卡孩子在哭，但是奥斯卡并没有出去把孩子领进来，于是人们就报了警。在纽约，父母不能将小孩子单独留在某个地方，这样做是违法的。

但奥斯卡说，在丹麦父母经常把孩子放在童车里，留在外面。孩子很安全，没人会伤害他们。丹麦人会互相照顾别人的孩子。他以为到了美国事情也应该一样。

两天之后，警方发现奥斯卡说的话没错。在丹麦人们确实让孩子自己待在那里。于是他们释放了他，他带着克里斯汀回到了丹麦。

---

arrest *v.* 逮捕；拘留
look for 寻找

wake up 醒来；起床
against *prep.* 违反（法律或规则）

32

Verbal Customs

I am a writer. My name is Julie. I am writing a book about wedding customs all over the world. I have an *acquaintance* named Shyla. She is a dancer. She lives in the United States, but she is from India. I *interviewed* Shyla about Indian weddings. She told me about Indian wedding clothes and gifts. I took a lot of notes.

After the interview, I thanked Shyla. I asked her if she would correct

言语的习俗

我叫茱莉,是一位作家,目前正在写一本关于世界各地婚俗的书。我有个熟人名叫希拉,是位舞蹈家。她是个生活在美国的印度人。我就印度的婚礼对她进行过采访,她对我讲述了印度的结婚礼服和馈赠的礼物,而我则做了大量笔记。

采访结束后,我向希拉表示感谢,并问她可否帮我修改一下我的笔记。她答应了,让我写完之后把笔记邮寄给她。

acquaintance *n.* 熟人;认识的人   interview *v.* 采访

my notes. Shyla said yes. She told me to mail my notes to her when I finished writing them.

I put my notes in an *envelope* and mailed them to Shyla the next day. I waited two weeks, but she never sent them back to me. I called her, and she apologized. I asked her again to mail back the corrected notes. She said yes, but nothing happened. I waited a few more weeks and called again. Again she said yes, but I never received the notes from her. After that, I was too angry to call her again.

Shyla promised to read Julie's notes and correct them. But she did not mean what she said. Shyla had to get ready for a dance *performance*. She had to teach the other dancers. She had to make the *costumes*. She was doing everything herself. She did not have time to read Julie's notes. Julie's request was impossible for Shyla.

Shyla said yes because she didn't want to say no. In Shyla's culture, it is *bad manners* to say no to requests.

第二天，我把笔记放在一个信封里邮寄给希拉。等了两个星期，但她一直没有给我还回来。于是我便给她打电话，她向我表示歉意。我再次请求她把改好的笔记寄回来，她也答应了。可是仍然毫无音信。我等了几个星期后又打电话，她还是说可以，但我一直也没收到笔记。从那以后，我气得也不想再给她打电话了。

希拉答应帮茉莉看笔记并修改，但其实她并不是这样想的。她既要准备舞蹈演出，还要给别的舞蹈演员讲课，又要做演出服，所有的事都要她一个人亲力而为。她实在没有时间看茉莉的笔记，茉莉的要求她不可能满足。

希拉答应说可以是因为她不想说"不"。在她的文化当中，对别人的要求说"不"是非常不礼貌的。

---

envelope *n.* 信封   performance *n.* 演出；表演
costume *n.* 表演服装   bad manners 不礼貌

33

The Hidden Meaning of Colors

My name is Ed. I manage a college *bookstore*. Once a year, students can bring their old *textbooks* to the bookstore. We buy the used books from the students. Later, we sell them again for a very low price.

This year I asked my student aide, Jim, to help me. Jim sat at a table and took the students' books. The students had to *sign* their names on a form.

颜色的寓意

我的名字叫埃德，是一家大学书店的经理。学生们每年有一次机会可以把他们的旧书拿到店里来，我们把这些用过的书买下，然后再以较低的价格卖出去。

今年我让我的学生助理吉姆来帮忙。吉姆坐在一张桌子后面收取学生拿来的书，他们要在一张表格上签上自己的名字，再拿着表格去收款员那里，由收款员把钱付给他们。

---

bookstore *n.* 书店
sign *v.* 签名

textbook *n.* 教科书；课本

Then they took the form to the *cashier*. The cashier gave them money.

Most of the students signed the forms and got their money. But some students just stood at the table. They looked upset. They didn't sign the forms. Jim was puzzled. He asked me what was wrong.

Jim put some pens on the table for the students to use. They were red pens. Some of the students were Korean *Buddhists*. These students were upset. In their culture, they write a person's name in red when the person dies. These students did not want to sign their names in red. Signing their names in red was like asking for death.

Ed explained the students' problem to Jim. Immediately, Jim *removed* the red pens. He put blue pens on the table. The students were *relieved*. They signed their names in blue and got their money.

大多数学生都签完名字，然后去领钱，但也有一些学生只是站在桌子前面。他们看上去有些不高兴，没有人签名。吉姆很迷惑不解，他问我这是为什么。

吉姆在桌子上放了几支笔让学生们用，而这些笔是红色的。有些学生是来自韩国的佛教徒，正是这些人感到不高兴。因为在他们的文化中，只有当一个人死后人们才会用红色来写他的名字。这些学生不愿意用红笔来写自己的名字，那样做就像是在寻死一样。

埃德把学生们的问题对吉姆做了解释。吉姆立即把红笔撤掉，换成蓝色的。那些学生如释重负。他们用蓝笔签好名字并拿到了钱。

---

cashier *n.* 出纳员；收银员
remove *v.* 拿走；取出

Buddhist *n.* 佛教徒
relieve *v.* 使解脱；缓解；缓和

34

The Hidden
Meaning of Numbers

My name is Rod Sterling. I work for the telephone *company* in California. Last year, we had a problem. Many people bought *cell phones*, and we needed more telephone numbers. When many people need new phone numbers, we have to create a new area *code*. An area code is three numbers that come before a regular

数字的隐义

我的名字叫罗德·斯特林，在加利福尼亚电话公司工作。去年的时候我们碰到了一个问题。当时许多人购买手机，于是我们需要更多的电话号码。而随着人们对新号码需求的增长，我们就要制定新的电话区号，区号是一个三位数，加在正常的电话号码前面，同一地理区域内的人们使用同样的电话区号。

---

company *n.* 公司
code *n.* 区号；编码

cell phone 手机

phone number. Everyone in the same geographic area has the same telephone area code.

We changed part of area code 818 to 626. But some customers in that area were unhappy. They *complained*. They sent letters. They made phone calls. They called people in the state government. They even called the *federal government* in Washington, D. C. ! We were stunned. We never thought people would object to the new area code.

The customers who complained were Chinese. They believe that the number 8 is lucky. Their old area code was 818. Two 8s in a phone number is extra lucky. It means *prosperity*.

Changing to 626 was bad. Add 6, 2, and 6—The total is 14. Many Chinese people *associate* the number 4 with death. They do not want a phone number that means death. The Chinese customers wanted the telephone company to change 626 back to 818. But the customers did not succeed. They had to keep the new area code.

我们把818区中的一部分号码改成了626, 可是当地的一些客户很不高兴, 纷纷打电话或写信来投诉, 向州政府报告, 甚至还向华盛顿的联邦政府举报! 我们惊诧不已, 从来没想到人们会对新的区号如此强烈地反对。

这些投诉的客户是中国人, 他们认为8是个吉利数字, 而他们原来的区号是818, 一个号码里有两个8更是好上加好, 意思是发大财。

把这个数字改成626就糟糕了, 因为6, 2, 6, 加在一起等于14, 很多中国人把数字4和 "死" 联系在一起, 他们不想要这样意义的电话号码。这些中国客户想让电话公司把626改回到818, 但是没能成功, 只好使用新的区号了。

---

complain *v.* 抱怨；投诉
prosperity *n.* 繁荣；富足

federal government 联邦政府
associate *v.* 联想；联系

35

Rites of Passage

My name is Wilf. I am a *photographer* from London, England. Last year, I went to the United States to take photographs of city parks. One Saturday, I was at Central Park in New York City. I noticed a large, happy group of people taking photographs in front of a *fountain*.

成人仪式

我叫威尔弗，是来自英国伦敦的一位摄影师。去年，我前往美国拍摄一些城市公园的照片。那是一个星期六，我来到纽约的中央公园，看到一大圈人正兴高采烈地在一座喷泉前面照相。

photographer *n.* 摄影师   fountain *n.* 喷泉

It was a *charming* scene—green grass, the falling water of the fountain, and eight very pretty young women. One of the young women wore a long white dress. She had flowers in her hair. The other young women wore pink.

I started taking photographs, too. I spoke to one of the people near me, "Did the wedding just finish?" He looked at me strangely and he asked, "What wedding?"

The *celebration* was for the young woman in white. It was her fifteenth birthday. Her family was originally from Mexico. Their celebration was a quincean era. This is the time when Mexican, Cuban, Puerto Rican, and other Central American girls traditionally become adults. A quincean era looks like a wedding. People wear formal clothes. There are many *guests* and there is a special cake. But there is no *groom*!

这是一幅多么迷人的场景啊——翠绿的草地，喷泉的流水，还有八位楚楚动人的妙龄女郎。其中一个姑娘身穿白色长裙，头上插着鲜花，其他的女孩子则穿着粉色的裙子。

我也开始跟着拍照，并问身边的一个人："婚礼刚刚结束吗？"他诧异地看着我，问道："什么婚礼呀？"

这个庆典是为了那个身穿白衣的年轻姑娘举行的，这一天是她十五岁生日，她的家庭是墨西哥裔。庆祝仪式名叫"quincean era"，是墨西哥、古巴、波多黎各还有其他中美洲国家中女孩传统的成人典礼。"quincean era"看上去就像是婚礼一样，人们都穿着比较正式的服装，宾客满堂，还有一个特殊的蛋糕，但是没有新郎！

---

charming *adj.* 迷人的；美丽的　　　　celebration *n.* 庆典；庆祝会
guest *n.* 客人；宾客　　　　　　　　groom *n.* 新郎

36

Business Practices

My name is Shig Ito. I live in *Tokyo* and I sell computers. One day, I went to a school where people learn English. I talked to the computer teacher, Mr. Wilson, about new computers for the school.

Mr. Wilson was from California. He was new to Japan, but he could speak a little Japanese. I handed him my *business card*. He took the card with one hand. With the other hand, he took a pen out of his

商场惯例

我的名字叫伊藤，家住在东京，是名电脑销售员。一天，我去一家英语学校，和那里的电脑教师威尔逊先生商谈他们学校购买新电脑的事。

威尔逊先生来自加利福尼亚，他刚到日本不久，但能说一点儿日语。我送上了我的名片，他用一只手接了过去，并用另一只手从兜里掏出笔来，当我向他讲述电脑价格时，他就在我的名片上写下我说的情况。我当

Tokyo *n.* 东京   business card 名片

pocket. Then, when I told him the computer prices, he wrote down the *information* on my card. I was surprised and *insulted*.

In Japan, there are strict rules for giving and taking business cards. Japanese people use both hands to give business cards to others. Japanese people also use both hands to take business cards. In Japan, people look at business cards carefully. Then they put the business cards away. People never put business cards in a back pocket. People never write on business cards. Mr. Wilson insulted Mr. Ito when he accepted the business card with one hand. He also insulted Mr. Ito when he wrote on the business card.

Mr. Wilson did not mean to insult Mr. Ito. He spoke some Japanese, but he did not know Japanese customs about business cards. Americans do not have strict rules about business cards. Americans give or take business cards with either hand. Americans may write on business cards. They keep business cards anywhere that is *convenient*.

时很是吃惊，觉得受到了侮辱。

在日本，递名片和接名片都有着严格的规矩。日本人用两只手把名片递给别人，接过来的时候也要用双手。人们会仔细看名片上的字，然后把它收好。没人会把名片放进裤子后面的口袋里，也不会在上面写字。而威尔逊用一只手接过名片，这对伊藤先生来说是一种侮辱，而在上面写字则又是一次侮辱。

威尔逊先生并非有意如此。他虽然会说一点儿日语，但并不了解日本人关于名片的习俗。美国人对名片并没有什么严格的规定，递接时用哪只手都可以。他们也可以在上面写字。他们把名片随意放置，只要方便就好。

---

information *n.* 信息   insult *v.* 侮辱
convenient *adj.* 方便的

37

The Name Game

My name is Melissa Gillis. I teach English in a high school in South *Carolina*. Roberto Vega is one of my students. In another class, I have a student named Alfredo Marino. They are both from El Salvador. Last month,

the teachers had Parents' Night at the high school. I met Alfredo and Roberto's parents, Mr. and Mrs. Marino. The two boys have the same mother and father! They are brothers but have different last names.

名字的习俗

我叫米丽莎·吉利斯，在南卡罗莱纳州的一所中学教英语。罗伯托·维加是我教的一个学生，在另一个班上有个学生名叫阿尔弗雷多·马里诺。他们都来自萨尔瓦多。在上个月学校举办的教师与家长见面会上，我遇到了阿尔弗雷多和罗伯托两个人的父母，马里诺夫妇。这两个男孩居然是同一对父母所生，两人是兄弟，却有着不同的姓。

Carolina *n.* 卡罗莱纳州

In many Latin American countries, people have two "last" (family) names. The first family name comes from the father. The second family name comes from the mother. The boys are actually Roberto Marino Vega and Alfredo Marino Vega. "Marino" comes from their father and "Vega" comes from their mother.

When the boys started school in the United States, they wrote their names on a form. In the space for "last name," they wrote "Marino Vega". But in the United States, people are not used to double last names. A woman looked at Alfredo's form. She understood that Marino was his first family name, his father's name. She *crossed out* "Vega". From that day on, his last name for school was Marino. Another person looked at Roberto's form. This person decided that Roberto's last name was "Vega", and crossed out "Marino". Suddenly, the brothers had different last names!

　　在很多拉丁美洲国家，人们都有两个"姓氏"。第一个姓来自父亲一方，而第二个则来自母亲一方。这两个男孩儿的名字应该是罗伯托·马里诺·维加和阿尔弗雷多·马里诺·维加。"马里诺"是父亲的姓，"维加"是母亲的姓。

　　当他俩在美国的学校报名入学时要填表格，在"姓氏"一栏里他们写的是"马里诺·维加"。但在美国人们并不习惯这种双姓，一位女老师看到阿尔弗雷多的表格，知道"马里诺"是他的第一个姓，也就是他父亲的名字，于是就把"维加"划掉了。从那天开始，他在学校的姓就成了"马里诺"。而另一个人看了罗伯托的表格，以为他的姓是"维加"，便去掉了"马里诺"。这一下两个亲兄弟就有了不同的姓氏！

---

cross out　删掉；划掉

38

Gift Giving

My name is Ray Dryden. I work in a big shoe store in *Boston*. One day, a woman came into the store with her son. He was about twelve years old and he was looking for shoes. He tried on many different pairs. Finally, he chose a pair of *sneakers*.

送礼物

我叫雷·德雷顿，在波士顿的一家大型鞋店工作。有一天，一位妇女领着她的儿子来到店里。那个男孩大约十二岁左右，试穿了很多双鞋，最后选中了一双运动鞋。

Boston *n.* 波士顿   sneaker *n.* 运动鞋

I told the mother the price. Then she walked away from me. She stopped another customer and asked her something. Then the boy's mother gave the other customer some money. The other woman came over to me and *paid for* the shoes. I don't think the two women knew each other. It was very strange.

The boy, Paulino, and his mother are from the Cape Verde Islands. These islands are in the *Atlantic Ocean* near the west coast of Africa. Cape Verdeans have a belief about shoes. If you give shoes to someone you love, that person will leave you. Paulino's mother loved her son. She did not want him to leave her. That is why she asked the other customer to pay for the shoes. The shoes were not a gift from Paulino's mother, so she would not lose her son.

我把价格告诉了那位母亲，然后她就走开了，来到另外一位顾客身边，说了些什么，接着把钱交给她，那位女士过来付了鞋款。我知道这两个人互相不认识，这件事真是太奇怪了！

这个男孩帕乌利诺和他的母亲来自佛得角群岛，群岛位于非洲西海岸的大西洋里。佛得角人对鞋子有一种迷信，认为如果你把鞋送给你爱的人，那个人就会离你远去。帕乌利诺的母亲非常爱自己的儿子，当然不想让他离开，所以请另外一位顾客替自己付钱，这样一来这双鞋就不是她送给帕乌利诺的礼物，而她也就不会失去儿子了。

---

pay for 为……付钱

Atlantic Ocean 大西洋

39

Gender

My name is Jan Riley. I find American homes for international students to live in while they go to college in the United States. One time, I had students from Korea, Taiwan, and Japan. I planned a *picnic* for them on *Independence Day*, the Fourth of July.

We went to a park and ate hot dogs, hamburgers, and watermelon. Later, I taught them a game called "pass the orange".

性别

我的名字叫简·莱利，我的工作是帮助一些外国学生来美国上大学时找到可以寄宿的美国家庭。有一次我接待了一些来自韩国、中国台湾和日本的学生。7月4日独立日那天，我为他们组织了一次野餐会。

我们去了一家公园，吃了热狗、汉堡包和西瓜等食物。然后我教他们玩一个名叫"传橘子"的游戏。

picnic *n.* 野餐   Independence Day 美国独立纪念日

The students sat in a circle on the ground. They sat in this order: boy, girl, boy, girl, and so on. A boy had to hold an orange under his *chin* and put it under the chin of the girl next to him. Then the girl had to put the orange under the chin of the boy on her other side. They could not use their hands. If a boy and girl dropped the orange, they were out of the game.

The students kept dropping the orange quickly. But they laughed a lot, so I thought that the game was fun for them. They played the game several times. A few days later, I heard that some of the students complained about the game.

The students were from countries where traditionally men and women don't touch each other *in public*. When the students passed the orange, they had to be very close to each other. Their faces had to touch. This made them *uncomfortable*. They laughed but they did not think the game was fun. The students were embarrassed. The game broke their cultures' rules.

学生们围成一圈坐在地上，按这样的顺序坐一个男孩儿、一个女孩儿、一个男孩儿、一个女孩儿，依此类推。男孩子要用下巴夹住一个橘子，递给旁边的女孩子，然后这个女孩子也用下巴把橘子再传给下一个男孩子。所有人都不能用手，如果有人弄掉了橘子，就被判罚出局。

学生们不停地把橘子弄掉下来，但他们笑得很厉害，于是我以为他们玩得很开心。他们又玩儿了几次。可是几天之后我听到有的学生在抱怨这个游戏。

在这些学生的祖国有一个传统，男人和女人在公众场所互不接触。当学生们传橘子的时候，他们不得不挨得很近，脸部难免碰在一起，这让他们很不自在。他们虽然笑了，但并不觉得这个游戏很有趣。这些学生心里觉得十分尴尬，这个游戏同他们的文化准则有所抵触。

---

chin *n.* 下巴   in public 公开地；当众

uncomfortable *adj.* 不舒服的；不自在的

Healing

I came to the United States from Russia about four years ago. I couldn't speak English. I had a bad *cough*, so I went to the hospital. The nurse came out and called my name, "Sergei Karpov." She asked me some questions, but I couldn't understand her.

治病

四年前我从俄罗斯移民来美国，当时不会说英语。一次我咳嗽得很厉害，就去了医院。护士出来喊我的名字："塞尔吉·卡尔波夫。"她问了我几个问题，但我没有听懂。

cough *n.* 咳嗽

She took me to a small room, and I met the doctor. He listened to my *chest*. Then he saw my back. He pointed to my back and said something. I didn't understand his English, but I knew what he meant. He wanted to know about the red circles on my back. I said, "Banki," but he didn't understand. The doctor shook his head. He looked upset.

The doctor called in a *translator*. The translator spoke Russian and English. She explained the circles on Sergei's back. The circles came from ten special glass cups, called banki. Russians use banki to treat bad chest colds and coughs.

她领我进了一个小房间，见到了医生，他给我听了听胸口，然后看我的后背。他指着我的脊背说了些什么。我听不懂英语，但明白他指的是什么。他想知道我后背上红色的圆圈是怎么回事。我说道："Banki"，但他不明白，摇了摇头，看上去有些不高兴。

医生找来了一位会说俄语和英语的翻译，她解释了塞尔吉背上红圈的来历。这些圆圈是用十个特殊的玻璃杯弄上去的，这种杯子叫"Banki"，俄罗斯人用它来治疗胸口疼痛和咳嗽。

---

chest *n.* 胸；胸口   translator *n.* 译者；翻译

Sergei's mother used these cups on his back. She heated the banki and placed them upside down on Sergei's back. She left the cups on his skin for five minutes. The cups cooled. This made extra blood come into Sergei's skin. Under the cups, Sergei's skin became red. Then Sergei's mother gently removed the banki.

Sergei went to bed. Usually, he felt better after his mother used banki to treat him. This time Sergei did not get better. He had *pneumonia*. He went to the hospital. The doctor gave Sergei *antibiotics*, and he got well.

塞尔吉的母亲把杯子加热，然后从上而下放在他的后背上，放置五分钟。杯子慢慢冷却，这使得更多的血液进入塞尔吉的皮肤里，于是杯子下面的皮肤开始变红。最后母亲慢慢地把杯子拿掉。

塞尔吉上床睡了一觉。通常母亲用"Banki"给他治疗以后病就会好多了，可这次却没有见效。他得了肺炎于是他去医院就诊，医生给他用了一些抗生素药，他开始好转起来。

---

pneumonia n. 肺炎　　　　　　　　　　　antibiotics n. 抗生素

Can You Give Me a Hand?

An *idiom* is a group of words with a special meaning. The words in the idiom do not have their usual, ordinary meanings. Together, the words mean something different. English is full of idioms. You know some already, and you will certainly learn more.

Many idioms *mention* parts of the body: the head, the hands, the

---

你能给我一只手吗？

习语就是那些有特殊意义的单词组成的句子。在习语中，这些单词用的不是它们通常的意思，而是有其他的意义。英语里有很多习语。你已经知道一些了，但还要了解更多。

很多习语和身体有关：如头部、手部、心脏等等。你或许会听到有人

---

idiom *n.* 习语；成语　　　　　　　　　mention *v.* 提及；提到

heart, and so on. You might hear someone say, "My brother's getting a big head." The boy's head isn't growing! A big head is an idiom. This boy thinks he's very important and special. His sister doesn't think he is. She says that he's getting too *confident*.

A friend might tell you, "Be careful. That girl has a big mouth. " The literal meaning is that girl's mouth is large. However, have a big mouth is also an idiom. Your friend means the girl talks too much or she tells other people's secrets. Your friend is giving you some advice: You shouldn't tell that girl any private information. You can't trust her to keep quiet.

说："My brother is getting a big head." 这个男孩的头并没有变大！"头变大"的意思是说，这个男孩认为他很重要并且很特别。但他的妹妹并不这么认为。她说这句话的意思是他太自负了。

一个朋友也许会告诉你 "Be careful, That girl has a big mouth. " 这句话的字面意思是 "那个女孩的嘴很大"。"嘴很大"也是一个习语。但是，你朋友的意思是，这个女孩话说得太多或她喜欢讲一些别人的秘密。你的朋友在给你建议：你不要告诉那个女孩任何个人信息。你不要相信她会保守秘密。

---

confident *adj.* 自信的

Take a guess at the meanings of these three sentences. Each sentence has an idiom. Each idiom mentions the heart but has nothing to do with the heart.

1. She knows the words to that song by heart.

2. My heart was in my mouth.

3. He has a heart of gold.

Did you *figure out* the meanings of the sentences? Here they are:

1. She can remember the words to that song very well.

2. I was very afraid.

3. He is very good and kind to other people.

猜一下下面三句话的意思，每个句子里都有一个习语，都提到了心脏，但意思和心脏其实毫无关系：

1. She knows the words to that song by heart.

2. My heart was in my mouth.

3. He has a heart of gold.

你知道这些句子的意思吗？它们的意思是这样的：

1. 她能记住那首歌的歌词。

2. 我非常害怕。

3. 他对别人非常友善。

---

figure out 弄明白；弄清楚

There are idioms in every language. A few idioms in your first language may be the same in English. For example, for some *Spanish* speakers, a heart of gold is the same in Spanish, un corazon de oro.

The meaning of an idiom isn't always clear. So perhaps you'll want to buy a dictionary of idioms. That might be a good idea. Just don't pay an arm and a leg for it.

在每种语言里都有习语。你母语中的某些习语可能和英语里的有些意思是相同的。比如，对一些说西班牙语的人来说，a heart of gold和西班牙语里的un corazon de oro意思是一样的。

习语的意思并不是总是一目了然。所以或许你想去买一本关于习语方面的词典。这是一个好主意，但是注意不要在这方面放太多的精力。

Spanish *adj.* 西班牙的

42

Songkran

In many parts of the world, a new year begins on the first of January. However, new year celebrations also happen at other times. The start of a new year *depends on* the traditions of a country, a culture, or a religion. There is also great variety in the ways people

celebrate. Some people go to church, eat special foods, or throw a party. In Thailand, people celebrate the new year in April, and they

---

泼水节

在世界的很多地方，新的一年都是从1月1号开始的。然而，新年的庆祝也可能在其他时间进行。新年在什么时候开始取决于一个国家的传统、文化还有宗教信仰。人们庆祝的方式也多种多样。有的人去教堂，有的人吃特殊的食物或是举行一次聚会。在泰国，人们在四月份庆祝新年，并且他们用水来庆祝。

---

depend on 取决于；视……而定

do it with water.

The month of April is extremely hot in *Thailand*. Maybe that is why water is important in the Thai new year celebration. Water helps people feel cool, clean, and fresh, and the new year is a time for a fresh start (a new beginning).

The name of the Thai New Year's celebration is Songkran. This holiday begins in the middle of April (the day depends on the moon), and it lasts for several days. People look forward to it, especially children. They get ready for Songkran by collecting water guns, *buckets*, and *hoses*. They want these things because during Songkran, they throw water at people. Children get each other completely wet. They throw water at adults, too. If you want to stay dry, you have to stay inside. Everybody who goes outside gets wet!

Jad Kanchanalak grew up in Thailand. She remembers all the fun

---

在泰国，四月份非常炎热。也许这就是为什么在泰国的新年里水是那么重要。水能让人们感到清凉、洁净和振奋。新的一年是一个新的开始！

泰国庆祝新年的活动叫泼水节。这个节日从四月的中旬开始(根据月亮定时间)，将持续好几天。人们特别是孩子都盼望着它的到来。他们准备了水枪、水桶和软管，要把水泼到别人身上。孩子们互相弄得全身湿透，他们也往大人身上泼水。如果你不想全身湿透的话，你只有待在房子里不出来。任何一个在外边的人都会变成"落汤鸡"！

贾德·坎察娜拉克是在泰国长大的，她记得泼水节上的所有趣事。

Thailand *n.* 泰国
hose *n.* 橡胶软管

bucket *n.* 桶；水桶

of Songkran. She says, "We always played outside in front of our house in *Bangkok*. I used to get wet and stay wet all day! Nobody really minded getting wet. Everyone expected it. It was part of the holiday fun."

Songkran has more serious traditions, too. For example, people make visits to temples, and many people visit older relatives. They go to see them to show respect, and they bring water with them. The water has flowers in it and smells very nice. The younger people *sprinkle* water on the older ones. The older people sometimes pour water over the younger ones, and they wish them good luck in the coming year.

Jad remembers, "We used to make one or two visits to relatives. Then my sisters and I were free to play. Songkran is a very happy time."

她说："在曼谷，我们经常在我们的房子前边玩。我已经习惯了一整天都是湿漉漉的！没有人在意。每个人都在期望着这样。这是节日乐趣的一部分。"

泼水节还有一些重要的传统。比如，人们要去参拜寺庙，去走访亲戚，带着水去以此来表达对他们的尊重。水里放有鲜花，闻起来味道很好。年轻人往长者身上洒一些水。有的时候年长的人也往年轻人身上泼水，以此来表达对来年好运的祝福。

贾德回忆道："我们通常拜访一两家亲戚，然后我妹妹和我就可以自由地玩了。泼水节是一个非常开心的时刻。"

Bangkok *n.* 曼谷

sprinkle *v.* 洒；喷洒

43

Québec's Winter Carnival

Winters in the city of Québec, Canada, are very cold. There is ice and snow all around. The days are short and the nights are long. It doesn't seem like much fun, does it? But the city is beautiful in the snow. For the people of Québec, it's the *perfect* time to celebrate. So they have a big party. It's the Québec Winter *Carnival*, and it's the largest winter festival in the world. It lasts for three

魁北克的冬季狂欢节

加拿大的城市魁北克的冬天非常寒冷，到处都是冰和雪，而且昼短夜长。这里看起来没有多少乐趣，不是吗？但是这个城市在雪里非常漂亮。对于在魁北克的居民来说，这是一个庆祝的最佳时间。所以，他们举办了一个大型的聚会。这就是魁北克冬季狂欢节。它是世界上最大的冬季盛会，要持续三周时间。

perfect *adj.* 完美的；最佳的   carnival *n.* 狂欢节

weeks.

There are lots of things to do at Carnival. You can walk around the city and see the fine stone buildings and the beautiful churches. You can watch *dogsled* races through the narrow streets. There are also *canoe* races on the wide Saint Lawrence River. If you get cold, choose one of Québec *excellent* restaurants and have a good hot meal.

Outside the city, you can go skiing or skating, or you can try to climb a wall of ice. You can even drive a dogsled yourself. At night, you'll be able to watch fireworks. Then afterwards, you can go to sleep in a hotel made of ice!

Yes, it's true. Outside the city, there is a hotel completely made of ice and snow. The Ice Hotel opens for business in January. It stays

---

在狂欢节上有很多事情可以做：你可以围着这个城市散步，欣赏那些精巧的石头建筑和漂亮的教堂，在狭窄的街道上看狗拉雪橇，还有在宽阔的圣劳伦斯河上举行的独木舟比赛。如果你觉得冷了，就找一家魁北克极好的餐馆，吃上一顿热乎乎的大餐。

在郊区，你可以去滑雪或滑冰，或去爬冰墙，甚至亲自去驾驶一辆狗拉雪橇。在晚上，你能看到烟花表演。接着，你可以在一家用冰做成的旅馆里睡上一觉!

是的，这是真的。在这个城市的外边，有一家完全用冰和雪做的旅

---

dogsled *n.* 狗拉的雪橇
excellent *adj.* 极好的；卓越的

canoe *n.* 独木舟

open for about three months. Its walls of ice are several feet thick. There is a bar inside the hotel with tables and chairs made of ice. Ten-year-old Bobby visited the bar with his father, and they ordered a couple of *soft drinks*. Their drinks came in glasses made of ice. While he was there, Bobby used one of the computers in the bar to send e-mail to his friends and relatives. People can even send photos of themselves at the Ice Hotel.

Perhaps you are wondering about the beds in this hotel. The beds are all made of ice, too. They have *deerskins* on top. The rooms

---

馆。这座冰旅馆在一月开始营业，时间会持续大约三个月。用冰做成的墙有几英尺厚。里面有一间酒吧，有用冰做成的桌子和椅子。十岁的波比和他的父亲参观了这个酒吧并点了两杯饮料，他们的饮料盛放在用冰做成的杯子里。同时，波比用他的电脑给朋友和亲戚发邮件，还可以在那里发送自己的照片。

或许你正在疑惑这个旅馆的床是什么样的。这里的床也是用冰做成的。床上有麋鹿皮床单。房间里的温度只有25华氏摄氏度(-5℃)，所以旅

---

soft drink 软饮料（不含酒精）   deerskin *n.* 鹿皮

are only about 25F (-5℃), so the hotel gives each guest a warm *sleeping bag*. Bobby and his father had to wear their hats to bed, too.

Maybe you'd like the chance to stay at the Ice Hotel. Does it seem to you like an interesting experience? Hundreds of guests stay there each year, but almost no one stays a second night. Maybe you would rather stay at a *regular* hotel, with a fine restaurant and nice warm beds. Either way, beautiful Québec has something for everyone during Carnival.

馆给每个客人一个温暖的睡袋。波比和他的父亲在床上还戴着帽子。

也许你喜欢有住在冰旅馆的机会，这不是一次很有趣的经历吗?每年有数百人住在那里，但是几乎没有人在那里呆第二个晚上。或许人们宁愿住在一家有好餐厅和温暖的床的普通旅馆里。不论是哪一种，魁北克的冬季狂欢节对人都是有吸引力的。

sleeping bag 睡袋   regular *adj.* 普通的；平常的

Celebrating a New Baby

What did your parents do to celebrate when you were born? Of course you can't remember, but maybe they have photos from a *ceremony* of some kind. People usually have ceremonies to *mark* important events in life. For example, there are wedding ceremonies. Getting married is an important event, and having

---

庆祝一个新生命的诞生

你出生的时候你的父母是怎么庆祝的呢?当然你不会记得，但也许他们会有一些庆祝仪式的照片。人们通常为了纪念生命中的一些重要的事情而举行一些仪式，比如结婚典礼。结婚是非常重要的一件事，孩子的出生也是。在大多数文化中，都有庆祝孩子出生的仪式或其他的传统方式。

---

ceremony *n.* 仪式

mark *v.* 纪念；庆贺

a baby is, too. In most cultures, there are ceremonies and other traditional ways to celebrate a new child in the family.

In the United States, the proud parents of a new baby often *decorate* their front door. It's an exciting time for them, and they want to share the good news with their neighbors. For example, they may put balloons on their door. Pink balloons mean the baby is a girl. Blue ones are for boys. New fathers used to *hand out* cigars to all their friends. Today, that tradition continues, but things are a little different. Only about 25% of American adults smoke now, so the cigars are sometimes made of chocolate.

People around the world often celebrate a new baby with some type of ceremony, perhaps a *religious* ceremony. This may take

---

在美国，那些骄傲的父母通常装饰大门，这对他们来说是一个令人激动的时刻。他们想同邻居分享这一个好消息。比如可能在门上挂上气球，粉色的代表孩子是个女孩，蓝色的代表是个男孩。新爸爸们会给朋友发放雪茄。如今这个传统还在继续。但是事情还是有一点变化，现在只有25%的成年美国人抽烟，所以有时换成了巧克力做的雪茄。

世界各地的人们用不同的仪式来庆祝孩子的诞生，也许用一种宗教仪式。这可能在一个婴儿出生几天或几个星期的时候进行。在韩国，在孩子

---

decorate *v.* 装饰；装点   hand out 分发
religious *adj.* 宗教的

place when a baby is a few days or weeks old. In Korea, there's a traditional ceremony on the baby's 100th day. In Mexico, many new parents *dress* their babies in special clothes and take them to church. In some African cultures, the family plants a tree.

New babies in every culture have one thing in common: they all need names. Sometimes the parents choose their baby's name before the child is born. However, a baby's name is not always the parents' decision. Sometimes the name depends on family traditions, and some babies get their names at religious ceremonies.

Parents in the United States sometimes put the news about their baby in the newspaper. For example:

一百天的时候有一个传统的仪式；在墨西哥，父母给他们的孩子穿上特殊的衣服并把他们带到教堂；在一些非洲国家，有些家庭会以栽树来庆祝。

对于新生儿有一件事在所有的文化中都是一样的：他们都需要一个名字。有时父母会在孩子出生前就把名字取好了。但是一个婴儿的名字并不都是父母决定的，有的时候这要取决于一个家族的传统。还有一些婴儿是在宗教仪式上获得名字的。

在美国父母有时会把他们孩子出生的消息登在报纸上，比如：

---

dress *v.* 给……穿衣

Smith, Michael James, Jr. Born July 4, son of Michael J. and Sarah Dean Smith of Deerfield.

This baby has the same name as his father. Michael is a very common American name. Other American parents want unusual names for their children. Apple Kaufmann has a very uncommon first name. She says, "My parents let my eight-year-old brother *name* me!"

The parents of new babies often receive presents. In the United States, friends send them cards, flowers, and baby clothes. Presents, celebrations—these things are great. But what do most new parents really need? More sleep!

小史密斯·迈克尔·詹姆斯在7月4日出生。他是迪尔菲德·大迈克尔和萨拉·迪恩·史密斯的儿子。

这个孩子和他的父亲有同样的名字。迈克尔在美国是一个非常普通的名字，有的美国父母想为他们的孩子取一个不同寻常的名字。埃博·库夫曼就有一个很不寻常的姓。她说："我的父母让我八岁的哥哥给我取的名字！"

孩子的父母经常会收到礼物。在美国，朋友送给他们卡片、鲜花还有婴儿的衣服。礼物、庆祝仪式——这些都非常令人高兴。但是那些父母们真正最需要的是什么呢？更多的睡眠！

---

name *v.* 命名；给……取名

Graduations

Imagine you're a *senior* and it's your graduation day. How do you feel? Are you happy about the end of classes? Or are you sad about saying good-bye to friends? Some seniors feel ready for new experiences. Other seniors are nervous about the changes ahead. However, most of them agree: Graduation is a time to *celebrate* with friends and have fun!

毕业

假如你是一个毕业班的学生并且就在今天毕业，你会有什么样的感受呢?是会对能够告别课堂而高兴呢，还是会因为要和朋友说再见而感到难过?一些毕业生已经为将来新的经历做好了准备；一些人则对将要面临的改变感到紧张。但是，他们大多数都一致认同的是：毕业是和朋友进行庆祝和娱乐的时候。

---

senior *n.* 毕业班学生   celebrate *v.* 庆祝；庆贺

At many U.S. high schools and colleges, seniors have a tradition of *pulling pranks*. Pulling pranks means causing trouble, but just for fun. A prank shouldn't hurt anyone. The idea is to surprise people and make them laugh. Seniors often pull their pranks at night, in secret. At one high school, teachers arrived on the last day of classes and found a big sign in front of the building. It said "FOR SALE." At another high school, some seniors took apart a *VW*, carried the pieces into the school at night, and put the car back together inside the library.

Graduation has a serious side, too. It's a big *milestone* in a person's life, so schools hold graduation ceremonies, or *commencements*. Commence means begin, and commencement

---

在美国很多的高中和大学，毕业生有搞恶作剧的传统，就是制造麻烦，但是只是为了开心，不能伤害任何人。它的目的就是让人们感到惊奇并且大笑。毕业生经常在夜里秘密进行他们的恶作剧。在一所高中，当老师们在最后一天来到学校后，发现在教学楼的前面有一个大牌子，上面写着"热卖中"。在另一所高中，一些毕业生将一辆"大众"车拆开，将零件在夜里偷偷地运到学校，并在图书馆里面将它组装起来。

毕业也有严肃的一面，它在人的一生中具有里程碑式的意义，所以学校要举行一些毕业仪式或毕业典礼。毕业意味着一个新的开始，在美国大

---

pull a prank 搞恶作剧
milestone *n.* 里程碑

VW *n.* （Volkswagon）大众汽车
commencement *n.* 毕业典礼

marks the beginning of something new. Most graduation ceremonies in the United States follow similar traditions. People expect to hear the usual commencement music, and they expect speeches by important guests. Some speakers tell jokes, but most talk seriously about the future.

People also expect to see the students all dressed in caps and *gowns*. Their teachers or professors wear similar caps and gowns. The colors that professors wear tell you about their work. For example, orange stands for engineering, light blue is for education, and purple is for law.

多数的毕业仪式都是相似的。人们盼望听到毕业进行曲，并希望能够听到那些贵宾的演讲。这些演讲者有时会讲一些笑话，但是大多数都是很严肃的，讲一些关于未来的事。

人们也希望见到学生们穿上长袍戴上帽子的样子。他们的老师或教授也穿同样的衣服，一位教授衣服的颜色会告诉你他的身份。例如，橘黄色代表工程学，浅蓝色代表教育学，而紫色则代表法律。

---

gown *n.* 长袍；礼服

The cap a student wears is called a *mortarboard*. A *tassel* hangs from the top of it. Before graduation, everyone's tassel is supposed to hang on the same side of the mortarboard. Then, immediately after a student receives his or her degree, the student moves the tassel to the opposite side. It's a strange tradition!

After the ceremony, students often do something else with their caps. They take them off and send them flying up into the air. How did this tradition begin? Who knows! But an old joke gives one answer: Why do graduates throw their caps into the air? Because their teachers are too heavy.

学生们戴的帽子叫作学士帽，它的顶部有一个流苏垂下来。毕业前，每个人的流苏都是垂在学士帽的同一侧的，一旦他们拿到了学位，他们就马上把流苏移到另一侧。这是一个很奇怪的传统。

仪式结束后，学生们通常还用学士帽来做另一件事。他们将帽子摘下来并将它们扔到空中。这个传统是怎么开始的呢?估计没人知道。但是一则笑话给出了这样一个答案：为什么毕业生要把他们的帽子扔到空中呢?是因为他们的老师太重了。

---

mortarboard *n.* 学位帽   tassel *n.* 流苏

46

Comfort Food

It's *natural* for people to eat when they're hungry. But people eat for other reasons, too. Do you ever eat because you're with friends and everyone else is eating? Do you ever eat because you feel tired, or because you are under stress? Many people do. People often eat to feel better. Maybe they have too much to do, or they're nervous. Maybe

---

安慰食品

人们饥饿的时候吃饭是很自然的，但是人们也会因为别的一些原因去吃东西。你有没有因为和朋友在一起，而他们都在吃，所以你也吃的时候？你有没有因为在感到疲劳或者有压力的情况下吃东西？很多人有过这种经历。人们经常为了感觉好一点而去吃东西，也许是因为他们有太多的工作要做，或者因为他们感到紧张；也许是因为他们的一个关

---

natural *adj.* 自然的；正常的

they're having problems in a relationship. But when people eat to feel better, they don't eat just anything. They want *specific* kinds of food. They want food that helps them relax. They want comfort food.

What is comfort food? For most people, it's food that is easy to *prepare*. It's often soft, so it's easy to eat. Eating it gives people a warm feeling. Sometimes it's a type of food that people loved as children. Maybe they used to eat it at specific times or places. Maybe it's food their mother used to make. Comfort food makes people feel "Somebody's taking care of me."

Researchers at the University of Illinois did a *survey* on comfort food in the United States. They asked over 1,000 Americans about

---

系出现了问题。但是当人们为了感觉好一点而去吃东西的时候，并不是吃什么都可以。他们想要吃特殊的食物。要那种能够帮助他们放松的食物，即安慰食品。

什么是安慰食品呢?对大多数人来说，就是那种方便准备的食物。它通常是软的，吃起来容易一些。吃这种食物给人一种温暖的感觉。有时会是那种他们小时候爱吃的东西，也许在特殊的时间或地点吃这种食物。也许是那种他们的母亲过去通常做的一种食物。安慰食品让人们感觉到"有人正在照顾我"。

伊利诺伊大学的调查员们做了一个关于美国安慰食品的调查。他们

---

specific *adj.* 特殊的　　　　　　　　　　　prepare *v.* 准备
survey *n.* 调查

it. They wanted to know two things: What comfort foods did people want, and when did they want them? The results of the survey were rather surprising. The researchers expected people's favorite comfort food to be warm and soft. But it wasn't. The number one food turned out to be potato chips. Another favorite was ice cream, especially among people aged 18−34. However, not all comfort foods are *snack* foods. Nearly half of the comfort foods were healthy, homemade foods, such as chicken soup and *mashed potatoes*.

People of different ages want different comfort foods. There are differences between the choices of men and women, too. The survey showed that American women usually choose sweet comfort

---

问了超过1000个美国人，想掌握两件事：人们需要什么样的安慰食品？人们什么时候需要它们？调查的结果非常令人吃惊。调查者以为人们的回答会是温暖的和柔软的食物。但答案不是。排在第一位的是薯片。另外一种最受欢迎的食物是冰淇淋，特别是那些年龄在18岁至34岁之间的人最喜欢。并不是所有的安慰食品都是快餐。近一半的安慰食品是有益健康的，自己家里做的食品，比如鸡汤和土豆泥。

　　不同年龄的人想要不同的安慰食品，男性和女性在选择上也有差别。调查显示美国的女性通常选择甜食，女性在这里面提到最多的就是冰淇淋

---

snack *n.* 快餐

mashed potato 土豆泥

foods. Women in the survey mentioned ice cream most often (74% of them like it), then chocolate (69%), and cookies (66%). Even more of the men in the survey mentioned ice cream (77%). However, men choose sweet foods less often than women. American men often want hot and salty comfort foods such as soup (73%) and pizza or *pasta* (72%).

When do Americans most want comfort food? Many people think it is only for times of stress, or when someone feels bored or lonely. However, the researchers say that the *opposite* is true. Yes, people eat to feel better. But more often, they eat comfort foods when they already feel happy. They eat them to celebrate or *reward* themselves.

(74%的人喜欢它)，接着是巧克力(69%)和小甜饼(66%)。在调查中甚至有更多的男性喜欢冰淇淋(77%)。然而，选择甜食的男性要比女性少。美国的男性通常喜欢热的和咸的食物。比如像汤(73%)和比萨饼或者意大利面条(72%)。

美国人什么时候最想要安慰食品呢？很多人认为只有在有压力的时候或者当人感到厌烦、孤独的时候。但是调查结果正好是相反的。是的，人们为了感觉好点而去吃东西。但更多的情况下是因为他们感到高兴才吃的。他们为的是庆祝一下或犒劳自己一下。

---

pasta *n.* 意大利面食

reward *v.* 奖赏；奖励

opposite *adj.* 相反的

47

Garlic

Some people can't stand *garlic*. "That smell! It's too strong. And it doesn't go away! There's nothing worse than garlic," they say. Other people say it tastes great and it's good for you, too. Chester Aaron grows eighty-seven kinds of garlic on his farm. He wrote a book called *Garlic Is Life*. It seems that people either love garlic or hate it.

大蒜

__些人忍受不了大蒜。"那种味道!太难闻了,并且总是挥之不去!没有比大蒜更糟的了。"还有一些人说大蒜很好吃,并且对你有一定的好处。查斯特·阿伦在他的农场种了87种大蒜,他还写了一本叫作《大蒜就是生命》的书。看来人们不是喜欢就是厌恶大蒜。

---

garlic *n.* 蒜;大蒜

Garlic has a long history. The first wild garlic probably grew somewhere in western Russia. People in that area found it and learned to use it. Later, travelers carried garlic with them to China, India, Europe, and North Africa. Farmers began planting it over 5,000 years ago. They grew garlic to eat and to use as medicine when they were sick. They also grew it for use in religious ceremonies.

People in many cultures shared similar ideas about garlic. For example, they made their slaves eat it. They believed garlic made it possible for slaves to work harder and longer. In *Greece*, the *athletes* of the first Olympic Games ate garlic. They wanted to become stronger and faster, and they believed that garlic would help. Soldiers in the Roman army ate garlic, too. They ate it to help them

---

　　大蒜有很悠久的历史，第一种野生大蒜可能是在俄罗斯西部地区出现的。人们在那里发现了它并学会了怎么去使用它。不久，旅行家们将它带到了中国、印度、欧洲和北非。在5000年前农民就开始种植大蒜，用它来做一种食物，并且在他们生病的时候当成一种药来使用，还在一些宗教仪式上用到它。

　　在不同的历史文化中，人们对大蒜有一些相同的观点，比如让奴隶吃大蒜，以为可以让他们长时间努力工作。在希腊举行的第一届奥林匹克运动会上，运动员们就吃大蒜。因为他们觉得大蒜可以让他们变得强壮并且提高他们的速度。罗马军队中的士兵也吃大蒜。大蒜使他们的战斗力更

Greece *n.* 希腊

athlete *n.* 运动员

fight better. But garlic wasn't only for slaves, athletes, and soldiers. In some places, garlic was called "food for lovers".

People had even more uses for garlic. They added it to other foods because it tasted good. In China, people also used garlic to keep meat fresh. The Chinese were probably the first people to write about the uses of garlic. They wrote about garlic 4,000 years ago.

People in many cultures ate garlic when they got sick. It *was supposed to* make a cold or *fever* go away. It was also supposed to help with different kinds of pain, for example, when someone's head, ear, or *muscles* hurt.

强。但是，大蒜并不只是给奴隶、运动员和士兵吃的，在有的地方，大蒜被称为"情人的食物"。

大蒜还有很多其他的用法，因为它的味道不错，人们就将它掺入到其他的食物里。在中国，人们还用大蒜为肉保鲜。中国人也许是世界上最早将大蒜的用法记录下来的国家，大约是在四千年前。

人在感冒时吃大蒜，很多地方都用这种方法，人们认为这样可以治疗感冒或发烧。大蒜还被用来治疗各种疼痛，比如头疼、耳朵疼或肌肉疼。

be supposed to 应该；被期望　　　　　　　　　　fever n. 发烧
muscle n. 肌肉

Is eating garlic actually good for you, or should we just laugh at these old ideas? The truth is, doctors today are telling their patients, "Eat garlic!" Recent research shows that garlic is good for your heart. It turns out that garlic helps people stay healthy.

However, we can't accept every idea about garlic from the past. In many cultures, people *trusted* garlic to protect them from all kinds of bad luck. Garlic is great, but it can't do that! Also, don't tie garlic around your neck. It won't keep *vampires* away, as people used to think. It would probably just keep your friends away.

吃大蒜真的对你有好处，还是我们应该对这些古老的想法不屑一顾呢?事实上，医生们给病人的建议是"吃大蒜"！最近的调查表明大蒜对人的心脏有好处。这说明大蒜可以保持人体健康。

但是，我们并不能认为过去人们对大蒜的看法都是正确的。在很多地方，人们相信大蒜可以让他们远离霉运，大蒜是好东西，但是它却没有这种功能!而且不要相信把大蒜挂在脖子上就可以将吸血鬼吓走这种说法，这样做只会把你身边的人给吓走。

---

trust *v.* 相信；信任   vampire *n.* 吸血鬼

Wedding Cake

Do you ever see American weddings in Hollywood movies? Those weddings aren't all exactly the same. They can *vary* in a hundred ways. But one thing never changes: There is always a wedding cake. You see it at the *reception* after the wedding ceremony. In the movies, the cake is always tall, and it's always white, like the long white dress of a traditional bride. On

---

结婚蛋糕

你在好莱坞的电影里看见过美国婚礼吗?这些婚礼都是不一样的,它们可能有上百种形式。但有一件事是一样的,每个婚礼都必须有一个结婚蛋糕。你会在婚礼仪式结束后的宴会上看到它。在电影中,蛋糕都很高并且是白色的,就像新娘穿的白色礼服一样。在蛋糕的顶

---

vary *v.* 不同;变化　　　　　　　reception *n.* 欢迎会;招待会

top of the cake, you'll probably see a little plastic bride and groom.

At a real American wedding, things won't be just like in the movies. The bride may wear blue. But there will *definitely* be a cake.

When did this tradition begin? The first wedding cakes were made thousands of years ago in Greece. A wedding cake at that time was more like bread. The *bride* had to make it herself, and it took her two days or more. Before she baked it, a child would throw a ring into it. Later, when people ate the bread, someone would find the ring. That person was supposed to be the next one to get married.

Most brides today don't bake their own cakes; they buy them.

部，你有时会看到一个塑料的新郎和新娘。

真正的美国婚礼和电影里的不太一样。新郎会穿着蓝色的衣服。但是婚礼上绝对会有一个蛋糕。

这个传统是从什么时候开始的呢?第一个结婚蛋糕是几千年前在希腊出现的。那时的蛋糕看起来更像是面包，新娘必须亲手制作，这往往要花新娘两天或更多的时间。在制作之前，要有一个孩子把一枚戒指扔到蛋糕里。当人们吃蛋糕的时候，如果谁吃到那个戒指，那么他就会被认为是下一个要结婚的人。

如今大多数新娘并不亲手去做蛋糕，而是买蛋糕。一些新娘要为此花

---

definitely *adv.* 肯定地   bride *n.* 新娘

Some brides spend a lot of money on them. A wedding cake can cost thousands of dollars. One woman ordered her cake from a famous cake maker 2,000 miles away. Her father sent his private plane to pick it up. The bride said, "I want my cake to be special! Nobody will remember the food at my wedding, but everyone will remember the cake."

When it's time to cut the cake, the bride and groom do it together. The bride uses a knife with flowers or pretty *ribbons* on it. The groom places his hand on hers. They cut the first piece from the bottom *tier* of the cake. The bride holds the piece, and the groom takes a bite.

费很大一笔钱。一个结婚蛋糕可能会花费几千美元。有位准新娘在两千英里外一个著名蛋糕师那里订购了一个蛋糕，她的父亲用私人飞机把蛋糕取了回来。这位新娘说："我想让我的结婚蛋糕与众不同!没有人会记得婚宴上吃了什么，但他们会记住这个蛋糕。"

在切蛋糕的时候，新娘和新郎要一起动手。新郎拿着带有鲜花或漂亮丝带的刀，新郎的手放在新娘的手上，从蛋糕的最底层切下第一块。新娘

---

ribbon *n.* 丝带   tier *n.* 层

Then he holds it while she takes the next bite. The bride and groom save the top tier of the cake and freeze it. They will eat it one year later, on their first *anniversary*.

Most guests eat their piece of the cake at the reception. But some people take it home in a box. That night, they put the box under their *pillow*. Why? It's another tradition. When they go to sleep, they're supposed to dream of the man or woman they will marry.

拿着这块蛋糕让新郎吃一口，新郎拿着让新娘吃一口。他们将蛋糕的最顶层冷冻起来，在结婚一周年的时候再把它吃掉。

大部分人会在婚宴上把蛋糕吃掉，但有的人会将蛋糕放在盒子里带回家。当天晚上，他们将盒子放在枕头下面。为什么这么做呢?这是另一种传统。当他们入睡后，他们会梦见将来的爱人。

---

anniversary *n.* 周年纪念日   pillow *n.* 枕头

Slow Food

Italians know and love good food. It's at the heart of their culture. They don't like to *rush* through meals, either. So, many of them think that fast food is a terrible idea.

In 1986, something happened in Italy. An American fast food restaurant—a McDonald's—opened in Rome. Many Italians were surprised and angry. They thought, "This is an attack on Italian

"慢餐"

意大利人了解并且喜欢美食，这是他们文化的核心部分。他们不喜欢仓促的饮食。所以很多人认为快餐是一个糟糕的主意。

1986年，在意大利发生了一件事。麦当劳——一种美国快餐，在罗马开了一家餐馆。这让很多意大利人感到吃惊和气愤，他们认为"这是对意大利文化的一种攻击！"一个叫卡罗·派垂尼的人决定对此进行反击。

rush *v.* 匆忙地做

145

culture!" One man, Carlo Petrini, decided to fight back. "Fast food is the *enemy*," he said. In 1989, Petrini started a group called Slow Food. Today, about 70,000 people belong to the group. They live in forty-five countries around the world. More people join every day.

The members of Slow Food have many ideas in common. There are a lot of problems with food today, they say. Fast food is one of them. For one thing, it's not healthy food. Also, it's the same everywhere. "That's boring," they say. They want to keep traditional cooking with all its variety.

Slow Food members worry about a second problem, too. Some types of plants and animals are getting to be very *rare*. They include, for instance, a kind of tree in Morocco, a special type of Austrian

---

"快餐是我们的敌人，"他说。1989年，派垂尼发起了一个名叫"慢餐"的组织。如今，大约有七万人加入了这个组织，他们分布在世界上四十五个国家，而且每天还不断有人加入。

"慢餐"的成员在很多问题上意见是一致的：如今的食物存在很多问题，快餐就是一个。问题之一就是它们不是健康食品，而且世界各地都存在这种问题。他们说："这很令人烦恼"。他们想保留那些各式各样的传统饮食。

"慢餐"成员也担心第二个问题：某些种类的植物或动物的数量越来越少。比如在摩洛哥的一种树，奥地利的一种特别品种的牛和美国的一种

---

enemy n. 敌人

rare adj. 稀有的；罕见的

cow, and wild rice in the United States. The world is in danger of losing them completely. Slow Food doesn't want to let them *disappear*, so they're working with farmers to keep them alive.

There's a third problem. Big companies produce much of our food today. They sell their products in many places, so they want products that can travel well. Big growers want the kinds of fruit and vegetables that look good after a long trip. But how do their apples, *lettuce*, and tomatoes taste? That's less important to them. So now we have more trouble finding good-tasting food.

Today, it's common to eat foods from far away. Food travels an

野生水稻。世界正面临着永远失去它们的危险。"慢餐"的成员们不想让它们消失，于是他们和农民一起为了它们的生存而努力着。

还有第三个问题。大公司生产我们需要的大部分食物。它们在很多地方进行销售，所以他们想让他们的产品更适于运输。大庄园主想让他们的水果和蔬菜在经过长途运输后看上去仍很新鲜。但是他们的苹果、莴苣还有西红柿尝起来怎么样呢?这个问题对生产者并不重要。因此我们现在想找到味道鲜美的食物很不容易。

disappear *v.* 消失

lettuce *n.* 生菜; 莴苣

average distance of 1,300 miles to reach dinner tables in the United States. In the past, people got their food from farms and factories in their local area. Slow Food members say, "People should buy more local food. It's fresh, and it's part of our culture." One American, Gary Nabhan, decided to try this. For one year, all his food came from plants and animals near his home in Arizona. One local animal is the *rattlesnake*. Nabhan ate that, too! In his book *Coming Home to Eat*, he says it tastes just like chicken.

Fast food is reaching more and more parts of the world. But Slow Food is getting its message to more and more people, too.

现在，吃到很远地方的食物是很正常的。在美国的餐桌上，食物平均被运输了一千三百英里。在过去，人们都是从当地的农场或工厂获取食物的。"慢餐"的成员说："人们应当更多地去买当地的食物，因为很新鲜，并且这是我们文化中的一部分。"一个美国人，加里·纳波汉决定对此进行一下尝试。在一年的时间里，他的所有食物都来自他的家乡亚利桑那。那里有一种蛇叫响尾蛇，纳波汉也把它当成食物。在他的《回家吃饭》一书中，他说这种蛇的肉吃起来就像鸡肉。

快餐正在世界上越来越多的地方传播。但是"慢餐"也正为越来越多的人所了解。

average *adj.* 平均的　　　　　　　rattlesnake *n.* 响尾蛇